Bullet Lists

Prof. Oddfellow

Saint Augustine

© 2022 by Craig Conley, writing as Prof. Oddfellow.

www.OneLetterWords.com

The Expression of Uncertainty

"I'm not sure about the muffins,"

not sure about the purple

not sure about the visualizing

not sure about the rest of my family.

not sure about the sushi.

not sure about myself.

not sure about the logic.

not sure about the connection between God and nature.

not sure about any of this.

not sure about now,

not sure about the future,

I'M NOT SURE ABOUT

WHY THINGS ARE GOING THIS WAY

not sure about anything anymore.

How We Did It...

The bullet lists collected in this book were mostly crafted from snippets encountered through the course of our research. We organized particular themes as we built the lists. The clippings on this page are a good example, though to save time along the way we tended to simply type out the snippets rather than clip them.

There's nothing to worry about because...

- it will automatically shut itself off.
- this is the new normal.
- all the testimonies have been shredded.
- you're in capable hands.
- you're not one of "them."
- all this is part of your dream.
- you can change your will as often as you like.
- nothing has been lost—just as nothing will be gained.
- you yourself are the eternal energy of the universe playing hide-and-seek with itself.
- things are much better than they used to be.
- it is so enormously complex that nobody is going to figure it out.
- Mother Nature will intervene somehow.
- you don't plan to do anything about it anyway.

Nothing changes until...

- we hit some kind of bottom.
- someone starts to dream.
- a complete power-down of the system.
- the soul changes.
- behaviors change.
- the players pick up the pieces and start a new game.
- the data is artificially changed.
- you actually quit.
- we ask ourselves questions.
- we shine a light on the issue.
- you make your voice heard.
- we get sick of ourselves.
- it's changed in everyone's memories.
- it becomes what it is.
- the next version comes out.
- a small cat appears.

The moon is actually...

- an egg that won't hatch for a long time.
- a big TV.
- older than the earth.
- not made of green cheese but rather mozzarella.
- a small planet.
- darker than the sky.
- a hollow alien spaceship.
- smaller than any star.
- a god.
- constructed of styrofoam.
- Hell.
- more strongly bound to the sun than to earth.
- silver.
- an oval.
- falling like a stone.
- a rather poor reflector.
- semi-transparent.
- orbiting within Lucifer's atmospheric envelope.
- rather pleasant.
- anything but a boring place.
- making our day a little bit longer every thousand years.
- the place of departed spirits.
- a museum world.

A cat never...

- acknowledges itself beaten.
- gives in totally.
- makes an apology.
- scratches without a good reason.
- feels ashamed of itself.
- forgives an injury.
- eats a cat.
- thinks it belongs to anybody.
- has nothing to do.
- has tender mercies.
- forgets being scruffed by its mother.
- can be over-indulged.
- leaves a home it has chosen.
- outgrows a love for play.
- tells a secret.

The very best thing is...

- good talk.
- being done.
- Hallowe'en.
- to answer not a word.
- an all-over bath with cool, not cold, water.
- an old-fashioned anise-seed tea.
- to go away from here.
- to be literary.
- just going to sleep.
- to begin again.
- not having to go to school.
- to do nothing.
- unencumbered, untrapped, unchained.
- that it will happen again tomorrow.
- that which must remain unwritten.

The only way forward is...

- politely but firmly to refuse.
- to forget the past.
- to first move backward.
- not to capitulate.
- to default and exit.
- acknowledgement and acceptance.
- to find the means to get out.
- through dialogue and reconciliation.
- to restore momentum.
- partnership.
- a lasting ceasefire.
- to disrupt.
- to depoliticize and demystify.
- mutual respect and understanding.
- to find a path that starts in the middle.
- to start walking.

The reason for everything is...

- there in front of you, wearing that cunning little yachting cap maybe.
- is never the logical conclusion.
- to point us to the meaning.
- we're all mortal.
- what it generates.
- luck.
- consciousness.
- that there is no reason for anything.
- nothing more than the proverbial tip of the iceberg.
- that it seemed like a good idea at the time.

Begin now because...

- to do the thing properly requires time and champagne, and at present neither are handy
- even those who have the highest hopes are worried
- things that you see around you will change
- the clock is ticking
- it looks like rain
- it is not going to go away
- we cannot afford to wait until a better technology comes along
- we will need all our imagination and our wisdom to cope with some of the critical moral questions soon to be thrust upon us
- the process can be long and challenging
- solutions will likely time time
- the risks are too grave and despite the associated difficulties, there is a great potential for good
- budget limits are already in place
- there's so much to cover tonight
- of the great amount of lead time required
- we have become totally morally decadent
- it will be easier now
- the longer we delay, the further behind we will fall
- the complexities start to snare you
- when we do recover we are going to recover because we put things on a sound basis
- it is a revolutionary time

The best thing to do is...

- buy a reset switch
- keep quiet about what you've seen
- acknowledge its presence and not get too worked up about it
- simply admit, "I don't know"
- be gentle with it
- dig a trench
- dangle a knotted rope
- use your newfound knowledge
- throw yourself into another activity
- yell and run for help
- limit your feelings by limiting your involvement
- stay cool and wait it out
- find out what works best for you
- keep at it
- say, "This is how it is, but there is no need for me to feel responsible and carry the whole burden"
- handle the matter personally
- calmly deny
- stay out of the middle
- expand the search area
- back up
- abandon it for another time
- ignore the stupid taunts
- smile, say "thank you," and move on
- start praying
- quit
- get on with your life

The only advice is...

- to let them alone; they will not change.
- practice controlling it, but keep it secret.
- eat and drink well, dance, and be merry.
- have nothing to do with it.
- to take one step at a time.
- try to observe with an unobstructed horizon.
- be prepared for the worst by avoiding it.
- that it's okay to be confused, and find some peace in your confusion.
- to follow you heart.
- that less is more.
- to stay loose.
- to use common sense.
- to emigrate.
- when you find the right stuff, buy in multiples.
- to let it be a little bit.
- to set aside everything you know (at least temporarily).
- go to bed immediately and stay there several days.
- to take no advice, to follow your own instincts, to use your own reason, to come to your own conclusions.

We may never understand...

- what happened and why.
- why dogs whine on car rides when they're the ones who begged to go.
- the senseless violence.
- if love just happens or is planned.
- the ultimate action of this or that agent.
- the religious and philosophical significance of the Japanese flowering cherries.
- all the details.
- the principle of universal love.
- the private logic behind Judy's behavior.
- how we will be changed by our long travels.
- why others treat us unfairly.
- how we arrived at our present condition.
- the deeper story, yet we know there is one.

The only thing left is...

- to get back to your bedroom.
- to untie the knot into a circle.
- to ask the moon for her compassion.
- the hard part.
- to enjoy the day.
- for the lawyers to clean up the details.
- to fly higher.
- to ask if it's worth it.
- a bunch of unanswered questions.
- to connect all the wires and turn it on.
- a little moody calm for a respite.
- surgical intervention.
- proving everything is independent.
- telepathy.
- to travel to Ararat.
- floating information.
- to liquidate and save what can be saved.
- the blood, some meat and the remains of magical power.
- a light.
- to proceed upon established lines.
- the space that includes the viewer.
- the unspeakable, the pure.
- some of their names.

The best thing in the world is...

- to get enough sleep.
- to lie on a soft rug before a fire.
- to laugh with a friend.
- to be got from books.
- flying at full speed from pursuit.
- to cultivate one's own garden.
- to be who you are.
- love.
- to have the heart of a child.
- individual freedom.
- to watch the day being born.
- work.
- a pile of nuts as high as a hill.
- to be self-forgetful.
- to be useful.
- laughter.
- to play music.
- to live; most people just exist.
- to know somebody needs you.
- in some cases, the very worst.
- always in danger of extinction.

We tend to forget...

- that even standing upright is a learned skill
- how much we are connected
- the middle items
- the sublime
- the liberating power of fantasies
- even those hard-won lessons that could help us solve recurring problems
- that a long-held assumption does not thereby become a fact
- things that do not fit our own personal expectations
- that the brain is not the mind
- how big an order of magnitude really is
- a great deal of what is said almost as soon as we hear it
- disagreeable experiences
- negative feedback about ourselvess
- how real the imaginary is to children
- about "us"
- that dogs are not people
- what we want to forget
- ourselves, forget we are in a theatre
- that the body understands the world in unique ways
- that it hasn't always been like this
- about those people that we do not know
- many things we knew when we were in the spirit world
- who we are

The best thing to do right now is to...

- get yourself a cookie
- proceed antisystematically and aphoristically, or lyrically, or musically
- keep together
- turn to page 8 and get an idea
- lay low for a bit and let the heat die down
- hold the nerves in, keep cool and let the fish take the line for a run
- bite the bullet and show up
- rest for a little bit
- keep quiet
- get away from the monkeys
- sit down, relax, have some lunch
- go for a swim
- build a fort
- give these people a chance
- get out there as quickly as possible
- just watch what he does
- learn how to cope on your own

How many ways can one get tossed aside?

An acquaintance discovered the following ways one can get tossed aside:

- Like a 7th grade boyfriend
- Like a forgotten dream
- Like a worn-out pair of boots
- Like a rag doll
- Like a useless bag of linseed
- Like a dog after his job was done
- Like a soiled tissue
- Like a dirty mop
- Like a master artist's sketch
- Like a broken appliance
- Like a taco wrapper
- Like a child's doll
- Like a piece of trash
- Like a wad of yesterday's news
- Like a used play thing
- Like a spent cigarette
- Like a sack of pork chops
- Like a Big Mac box
- Like a fat pedestrian
- Like a fad
- Like a goddamn rubber glove
- Like a moldy beanbag chair
- Like a dirty napkin

Nothing can go wrong if...

- there are backup systems.
- you don't get caught.
- you do it right.
- the eternal truths are stated loudly.
- you figure things out carefully.
- gold is near.
- you keep your head and listen to me.
- fate is on your side.
- you don't panic.
- you devise a strategy.
- we all stick together.
- you just treat X and Y as constants.
- we operate strictly according to plan.
- you practice what you have learned.
- your harness is sound.
- these people don't get elected.
- everything goes right.
- you just return to Paradise Island.

There is comfort in...

- having a good bed in a fireproof hotel.
- reflecting that it might have been worse.
- knowing we are not alone in our anonymity.
- a mother's caress.
- a stranger.
- the strength of love.
- the knowledge that evil is but temporary.
- the perception that we are all in this chaos together.
- using a procedure that gives definitive answers from confusing data.
- business as usual.
- the womb.
- being with those with whom we have spent pleasant and meaningful days.
- knowing the impermanence of all these conditions.
- church light, which is star light incarnate.
- the knowledge that the other shore has already been reached.
- a circumscribed life.
- numbers.
- a hermetic, tidy account of the past, and comfort too in a measured and recognizable voice, leading us through those long ago and lost intricacies.

The only way to survive is to...

- write and read big fat books
- make fun of yourself
- pretend you're not there
- embrace the madness
- run forward as fast as you can go
- be merciless
- work until the wee hours of the morning
- set yourself in perpetual opposition to the system
- gird your heart
- fight back
- become strong
- prevent
- join the side that's winning
- live underground and eat worms
- muster the aid of magic
- laugh
- hunker down
- become more efficient
- be one step ahead
- keep moving
- stay resilient in your suffering
- be totally self-seeking
- stick together
- climb out of the ring
- have a protest strategy from day one
- remove the brain implant
- actually be optimistic and make the best of everything
- stay connected

Sometimes a full moon...

- casts eerie shadows across tombstones.
- can create a rainbow at night.
- appears twice in the same month.
- peeks around the clouds.
- moves through the earth's shadow.
- looks so big and bright and magical.
- dances through gaps in dark clouds.
- makes all the difference in the world.

Nothing is true ...

- in Washington until officially denied
- especially in charcoal
- but that which rings of right
- and everything is permitted
- but the brutal, the vulgar and the vile
- in the false, cruel sea
- and anything is possible
- and nothing is eternal
- until it is discovered for oneself
- or what is true is not evident to us
- but falsehood
- but Heaven; nothing sure excepting sorrow
- is a logically untenable statement (the phrase destroys itself)

All you need is...

- a plunger
- a mirror and a good flashlight
- a piece of paper
- a spirit of adventure
- a quart of paint
- one unsuspecting subject
- a sheet you can spread under a tree
- a fertile mind
- desire and a little practice
- a piece of string about four feet long
- a flat playing area
- someone to trust
- a library card
- a bit of imagination and a sewing machine
- a little olive oil and diced garlic
- time
- fifty lucky breaks
- a good lawyer
- a good laugh

If only everyone would just...

- let me get on with it.
- do as they say.
- mind their own damn business.
- stand in silence and let the waves settle to flatness.
- forgive, the world would be a much better place.
- take care of themselves and let me live my life.
- think more clearly about what they are doing.
- pretend all is well and fine.
- relax, slow down and take it easy.
- sit down and talk, things could be settled.
- say "Yes" to whatever is before them.
- occasionally consider using the brake pedal.
- love everybody, these age-old riddles would be solved.
- wake up out of their bad dream.

The truth is that...

- even granite changes over time.
- if it were easy, everyone would do it.
- life itself is music.
- I was never that girl in the hallway.
- learning to laugh at yourself can help you.
- there is no "right" age for being who you are.
- there are so few who know where Burma is.
- a journey is an extension of the human personality.
- our body is in many ways like a robot.
- none of us has reached that exalted position of perfection.
- mind and matter are complementary to each other.
- sometimes what is supposed to be observable is lost in our focus on the flame.
- there is nothing noble in being superior to somebody else.
- your death would be something to fear only if you could survive it.
- teams often create negative synergy.
- it is okay for one or a few people to pee in a river, as the river's ecosystem can cope with that amount of pollution quite easily.
- the horse may be thirsty but not have the will to drink.
- everyone who trusted Jesus in the first century A.D. died.
- no one has a clue.
- love is the greatest thing upon this earth.
- there never is just one truth.

The thing to do is...

- once you've bloomed, hold on.
- change the course.
- keep up your spirits in spite of everybody and everything.
- get rid of the poison while it is still only on the surface.
- just laugh it off.
- begin while the infestation is slight.
- go back to doing what you do best.
- accept this madness of yours as a basic fact.
- keep occupied.
- face the worst with serenity.
- heed them both.
- be forever losing yourself in the enjoyment of embracing life.
- find a house and wait for Santa.
- play this game simply for the pleasure of playing it.
- accept this fact and try to utilize it.
- start before it's too late.
- the thing that can be done.

The only solution is to...

- sprout a pair of wings
- phase out the signal
- make the bucket bigger
- turn the machine off and leave it alone
- sedate them
- involve the community
- be disconnected and re-dial
- destroy the system and start all over again
- lighten the load
- make your home appear to be untenanted
- replace the damaged piece
- overthrow it and then poof... that's it
- abandon the dogmatic idea
- re-write the subroutine with higher precision
- grin and bear it
- prove them wrong
- drop the notion of total divine inspiration
- invent something different
- make the best of the material at hand
- limit the amount of information available
- accept the defeat and wait quietly for the positive forces to lead you
- reboot the system
- stop talking altogether and uses sign language
- do a backup for yourself
- travel off somewhere away from everyone

We can get through this if we...

- don't pass out
- stay in the moment
- tough out the next few days
- tell ourselves we can
- stay here and focus
- don't panic
- take risks
- trust each other enough
- do it together
- talk to each other
- keep our minds clear
- put up a united front
- follow simple precautions
- rely on the Lord
- vote on an amendment
- keep it light
- hold onto our patience
- stand up for one another
- can forgive
- are determined to grow
- don't start screaming

July is the month...

- to promote yourself
- of freedom
- of song
- of roses
- of great variety
- of the tempest's power
- for threshing
- of vacations
- of the least bird movement
- of transition
- of the insectivora
- for proverbial meteorology
- of patriotism and revolutions
- when the wooden spoon begins to get busy
- of the ruby
- when things really heat up in Copenhagen
- when fuchsias come into their own

Sometimes the smartest thing...

- cannot be defended intellectually
- is to let it roll off your back
- is to wait until next year
- is take on a humble task that needs doing
- is to give up and try from a completely different point of view
- is to shut your mouth and listen
- is to get out early
- is to apologize
- is to play along
- is to give up
- is to stop it altogether
- is delegating
- to bring to a gunfight is a knife
- is to go with the flow
- is to stay out of the way
- is to cut your losses
- is to be scared
- is to follow your heart
- to turn a complete about-face and offer something in total opposition to a trend
- is pack up, jump on your horse and gallop off to greener pastures

It's been said that everyone secretly wishes for something

- The gardener himself secretly wishes for a frost, though it isn't quite cricket to come right out and say so.
- Abby secretly wishes for "a hundred rainbows."
- Lisa secretly wishes for real problems, so that she can have something to complain about.
- At one time or another, everyone secretly wishes for more time or an extra pair of hands.
- Every man secretly wishes for a troublesome wife upon which to blame his failings.
- Every mom secretly wishes for a little more time on her side, a stolen moment to relax.
- Every pet owner who has had the misfortune to put down a pet secretly wishes for some sign from above that he or she has done the right thing.
- The fearful ones secretly wish for the entire world to be as helpless as they perceive themselves to be.
- Each of us, at times, secretly wishes for more personal fulfillment.
- Each side secretly wishes for a doomsday scenario in the misguided belief that their side will be proved "right."
- And although everyone secretly wishes for change in one or more bodily features, peace is discovered in a genuine love for one's self.

Things beyond compare

- the taste of yeast
- the world
- Paris
- the moon
- the human figure
- the sense of accomplishment
- Yahweh
- thy destiny
- the excellence of Italian cookery
- the beauty of a rose
- a blue-sided, white-capped mountain, reflected in a broad, placid, shimmering lake, and framed between fleeting clouds, graceful trees and verdant lawn

May we never forget...

- the Alamo
- why we are so happy
- the mystery of probability
- our heritage
- to take care of Mother Earth
- that music is magic
- what we owe to our heroes
- from whence we came
- there may be squalls (of temper as well as wind)
- the struggles and wants of the poor
- our vows
- the price of liberty
- the sacrifices of others
- the inscription on the Greek temple: "Know Thyself."
- our mortality
- that we are one people
- the wonderful power of kind words, kind actions, kind attention, and gentle treatment
- to use our voices, our time, our energy to make this a better place to be
- that every subject has many different aspects
- that archeology is about people and their behaviors, in all their marvelous, often bewildering, variety
- that professional courtesies are due to every honorable dentist
- the one thing necessary
- this joyous day
- how to laugh

It all comes down to...

- what works best for you
- your incredible insecurity
- the individuals involved
- coaching
- a failure to execute
- money management
- a simple choice
- being a coward
- how much weight a name will carry
- behavior
- emotional chemistry
- how you spin it
- hitting a key on the computer
- forming a word
- freedom and choice
- rhythms
- what you know and what you don't
- using your brain
- trusting your gut
- this election
- desire
- dedication
- finding your market
- higher aspirations
- memory
- negotiation
- safety

- character
- what you're throwing out
- blood
- human beings
- one girl
- attitude
- priorities
- accepting responsibility
- which way you pass the butter
- greed
- trust
- control
- whether you want your life to be full of accomplishments and triumphs, laughter and good times, or anger and frustration, bitterness and disappointments

The only way to be happy is to...

- live in the Now
- choose, moment by moment, your future
- make others so
- be of use in the world
- expect to have your heart broken every day
- shut yourself up in art
- be busy
- be humble
- wish to be happy
- behave like what you are
- love
- tolerate uncertainty
- restore inner peace
- forgive
- emancipate from guilt
- aspire to a higher purpose
- wonder
- start yourself over and over again

The problem with people is...

- inherent shortsightedness
- fickleness
- inability to communicate
- they're not all the same
- self-centeredness
- a lack of foresight
- overspending
- an unwillingness to pay their dues
- focusing on the destination instead of the journey
- taking themselves too seriously
- apathy
- inefficiency
- inattentiveness
- prioritization
- fear and confusion
- they make poor gods
- bargain hunting
- giving up too easily
- taking shortcuts
- an infinite supply of wants
- making small talk
- being only human

The only hope for recovery is...

- permanent separation
- admitting defeat
- prompt intervention
- a miracle
- early removal
- through collective action
- the tome of the watchtowers
- to drop the tyrant role
- pastoral counseling
- the guardians of the veil
- long-term analytic therapy
- to add maximum power and increase the angle of attack to the maximum lift condition
- to discover better living through something other than chemistry
- to find someone named Juan or Juana who was born on June 24th

The single most important thing is...

- to learn to stop
- to make sure the right people are in the right place at the right time
- not to thrust or over accentuate
- to be on time
- the song itself
- to protect the key remaining pieces
- to turn back and retake the road badly chosen
- to follow your dream
- to be observant
- to get communications working better
- that the trustee not be a friend or relative
- not a single thing but many little things
- that image has got to be right
- to really know your boat
- location
- long-term agreements
- to keep accurate records
- the personal touch—being flexible and accommodating
- blind, stupid, tunnel-vision self-confidence
- not to reveal your password
- the ability to figure out what is wrong
- to rely very heavily on self-help, self-initiated efforts
- to understand what the new realities of your society are
- you, then your outfit

The only place to go is...

- around in circles
- the next scary and uncomfortable place that fits who we've become
- within
- Mars
- up the wall
- a saloon
- outer space, with beep-beep robots and people covered in long fur
- back to Texas
- the cliff
- a sanitarium
- around the bend
- back to the alcohol or drugs
- abroad
- down to the floor
- back to some less exalted things
- back where you came from
- the abyss
- backwards
- to the movies
- a gay bar
- forward
- into the sensuality and stillness of the present moment
- small claims court
- back home in your own mind

- one of Jupiter's satellites
- deeper
- glorious and exuberant ruination
- into the pit
- toward the center
- somewhere out there to a Higher Source and to ask for supernatural help
- somewhere else
- further into the land of infinite recession
- to the place of perfect measure—the place that doesn't exist, at least not at present
- the local shrine
- back to the drawing board
- to a night the autumn before everything changed
- back to the beginning and enjoy it all again

The only thing left is to...

- color the outlined spaces
- gather up odds and ends here and there
- attack before dawn
- connect all the wires, turn it on, and hope it works
- ask the moon for compassion
- give up
- fly higher
- accept responsibility for your actions
- get back to your bedroom
- repair
- make conditions that they can meet
- proceed upon lines already established
- cure what might have never occurred
- fight to the very death
- dispose of the body
- soften the sharp edges
- untie the knot into a circle
- try to broaden its significance
- be sorry—humbly, bitterly sorry—and swear never again to be unkind—never never never again—until the next time
- play intensely
- work out a dignified way to come down
- make sure that whoever you show it to can read it

The only thing to remember is...

- to keep dodging at random
- change the subject completely
- that what works best for you is what works best, period
- not to move when danger is near
- what should be left undone
- to buy flowers and buy them as often as possible
- that, God bless them, they are vulgarians
- that you must take sensible precautions, most of which are blindingly obvious
- that whatever you do to one side of the equation, you must also do to the other
- to go totally
- that you have to cock the hammer before you squeeze the trigger
- to run faster than the other person; that's just good enough
- that bad points will be emphasized just as strongly as good ones
- to keep it free of lumps
- that if you want to double back on yourself it takes a bit of time to cancel out your inertia
- to keep the decimal points aligned
- to speak idea-wise, not sentence-wise
- that both history and future are only propositions and descriptions - the only real action is now
- to subtract backward
- if you love then all sacrifice is okay
- prompt treatment often saves much suffering

- never to look directly at the sun
- that you can't be half right
- self-preservation
- the Tetragrammaton
- to keep the shape fairly simple
- that there are no rules
- that a limp carrot is a very old carrot
- that the primary motivation comes from the familiar properties of "less than or equal to" and not "less than"
- a bond is created as soon as the pieces touch each other
- don't fly too close to anything else
- the old principle of harmony
- that we all put on an act from time to time, but there is no point in putting on an act before God
- memory cannot be taken as literally true
- that personal gains should neither be contradictory to divine rules nor cost losses to others
- not to set the voltage on the transformer too high
- don't commit the same mistakes again and again
- to be balanced between activity and inactivity
- you've got to win the war
- not to give too much
- to remain a witness
- to take a sure aim
- that souffles wait for no one
- the honesty, the sincerity
- to make sure the calculator is in the right mode
- you're the one who's supposed to be on top

- not to overdo it
- that it isn't and can't be November
- that "you were looking for a job when you found that one."
- never to waste a potential source of food
- when it's long, use the length
- be alert
- to make more than you think you will need
- don't become the mask
- to always demand to speak to someone in charge who is high enough up to be able to make spontaneous decisions on your behalf
- don't be worried about others' motivations
- not to apologize and to wear something white
- that being innocent and appearing innocent are two entirely different things
- the silence, the equilibrium, the balance, the integrity
- it is usually best to "start small"
- never to lose sight of the basics
- that you can't turn back on yourself
- to look up and not look down
- always be a lady, no matter how bad it hurts
- that you must act young and innocent
- that once you start giving prizes away, if you stop them, you're apt to stop the flow of questions
- don't expend all your creative energies trying to get comfortable
- stay away from the front windows and don't put any lights on
- not to meet their approaches with a similar rebuff

- if you're going to wait, you'll wait, and if you aren't, you weren't ever in love anyway
- that we have to speculate, if we are to have a rule for our conduct at all, that in one sense life itself rests on speculation, since it is always directed to ends not yet realized—so that the practical question is hardly whether we shall speculate or no, but whether we shall speculate wisely, comprehensively, consistently and well
- not to take yourself too seriously
- dreams
- that if you like it as much as I do make a bit more to allow for eating some as you go along
- that when you cross a field and go through a gate, leave the gate as you found it. That is a cardinal rule; do not forget it

Here's all you have to do

- All you have to do is listen. (Rob Kapilow, 2008)
- All you have to do is ask. (Meredith Walters, 2007)
- All you have to do is be the middleman. (Jay Abraham, *Getting Everything You Can Out of All You've Got*, 2000)
- All you have to do is win. (Trent Frayne, 1968)
- All you have to do is glance at your calendar. (Savitri Ramaiah, *Lifestyle During Pregnancy*, 2003)
- All you have to do is balance your weight. (Edwin Burford, *Skiing Made Simple*, 2007)
- All you have to do is share your experience, strength, and hope. (Robert Perkinson, *The Gambling Addiction Patient Workbook*, 2003)
- All you have to do is select items from a series of menus and the system does all the work. (Dinesh Maidasani, *Comprehensive Information Technology*)
- All you have to do is walk out your front door. (Howard Wimer, *Inner Guidance and the Four Spiritual Gifts*, 2014)
- All you have to do is to hit the RIGHT target with the RIGHT weapon at the RIGHT time. (J. C. Kemmerer, *Tournament Sparring*, 2011)
- All you have to do is be open. (J. K. Ellis, *Perfected Mind Control*, 2006)
- All you have to do is to make it happen. (Terence Hamilton-Morris, *Spirit Rises*, 2013)
- All you have to do is cut your calories and watch what you eat. (Dag Albright, *Chicks*, 2007)
- All you have to do is list what you want out of life and then sign your name at the bottom. (*Alternate Gerrolds: An Assortment of Fictitious Lives*, 2013)

- All you have to do is think properly. (Charles Mangua, *Son of Woman in Mombasa*, 1986)
- All you have to do is sort out your own theory of direct mail. (Tony Attwood, *Education Marketing*, 2005)
- All you have to do is be still and tap into the energy. (Danielle Garcia, *Angel Blessings*, 2008)
- All you have to do is put that down. (Zane, *Infinite Words*, 2015)
- All you have to do is live the life. (Angus Buchan, *Now is the Time*, 2014)
- All you have to do is decide what you want to change. (Nevaeh Michael, *Fall in Love Again*, 2012)
- All you have to do is start. (Leo Babauta, *Zen to Done*)
- All you have to do is send people to the offer and hope they buy. (Tracy Repchuk, 31 *Days to Millionaire Marketing Miracles*, 2013)
- All you have to do is change your thoughts. (Theron J. Houston, *I Once Was Lost*, 2009)
- All you have to do is have Ralph watched when he comes into your city. (Jeff Inlo, *Soul View*)
- All you have to do is state firmly but in a friendly manner, "No thanks, I have other plans." (*Keys to Learning*, 2007)
- All you have to do is get out of your comfort zone and be ready for new experiences. (Romy Miller, *How to Be the Man Women Want*, 2009)
- All you have to do is find a sheet of words, the words being colours. (Michael Robinson, 10 *Ways to Enhance Your Mind and Become More Efficient*, 2013)
- All you have to do is sit back and wait for the money to start rolling in. (*Marketing Your Ebook*)

- All you have to do is work backwards and precisely calculate what has to happen to make that journey. (*Getting Everything You Can Out Of All You've Got*, 2013)
- All you have to do is circle all that apply. (S. F. Berk, *The Gender Factory*, 2012)
- All you have to do is simply attend. (Jonathan C. Smith, *Relaxation, Meditation, & Mindfulness*, 2005)
- All you have to do is believe, let go of the past, and move forward! (Tammy Lynn Robinson, *Thoughts of the Heart*, 2013)
- All you have to do is show up. (Nancy Whitney-Reiter, *Now is the Time to Do What You Love*, 2009)

There's only one rule

- there are no rules (if you're stretching your imagination) —David Goss, *The Science of Living Better Forever*
- step on a crack , break your mother's back (if you're playing a sidewalk game)
- have the teapot in front of you at all times (if you're crocheting tea cosies) —Loani Prior, *Really Wild Tea Cosies*
- no deep-fried foods (if you're throwing a party and watching your cholesterol) —Mary Mihaly, *The Complete Guide to Lowering Your Cholesterol*
- there's no being tired (if you're touring Paris) —Penelope Rowlands, *Paris Was Ours*
- say "Thank you" (if you're receiving a compliment) —*Thriving in the Workplace All-in-One For Dummies*
- the teddy bear stays in the house (if you're a dog in training) —*Heavenly Humor for the Dog Lover's Soul*
- never, ever let a boy touch you there unless he's your husband —Gillian Flynn, *Dark Places*
- wear whatever is most comfortable (if you're hiking with a dog) —Dan Nelson, *Best Hikes with Dogs Western Washington*
- ever miss paying your round (if you're drinking with friends) —Jack Kahane, *Memoirs of a Booklegger*
- there must be at least one [item] on the list that is impossible (if you're setting goals) —David Taylor, *The Naked Millionaire*
- if you represent the wife, get as much as possible; if you represent the husband, give away as little as possible (in divorce settlement) —Howard K. Irving, *Children Come First*

- anything goes, as long as you keep at least two tires on the pavement (if you're driving an automobile) —Glenn Beck, *The Overton Window*
- conquer at any price (if you're on the battlefield) —Luis M. Rocha, *The Holy Bullet*
- yes means yes and no means no (in the sexual marketplace) —Glenn T. Stanton, *Secure Daughters, Confident Sons*
- never get involved with a student (if you're a good teacher) —Hank Brooks, *The Inlet*
- form, structure and content should not be separate (in synaesthetic cinema) —Simon Rycroft, *Swinging City*
- don't eat from the tree of knowledge of good and evil (if you're in the Garden of Eden)
- you need one equation for every unknown (in algebra) —Norman S. Pratt, *Pearls for the Moment*
- don't hit the ducks (in a joke about a golf course in heaven) —Stephen Motway, *Jokes, Quotes, and Other Assorted Things*
- the fewer attachments and aversions you have to the goal, the quicker it will manifest (if you're a non-dualistic self-inquirer) —Aleksander Kupisz, *Holistic Creation and Focus Zone Chi Gong*
- no touching of the net (if you're a volley ball player) —Joseph A Bulko, *Wall of Illusion, Book 3*
- you clean up after yourself down there (if you're in the kitchen) —Jennifer Taylor Wojcik, *From Day One*
- learn to listen (if you're training to be a good communicator) —John Mason, *Believe You Can*

Perhaps Andy Warhol Was Wrong, For a Fascinating Variety of Reasons

Andy Warhol famously predicted that in the future, everyone would be famous for fifteen minutes. Now that the future is already here, there are those who beg to differ with Andy, and for a fascinating variety of reasons!

In his novel *Rant* (2007), Chuck Palahniuk suggests that "Andy Warhol was wrong. In the future, people won't be famous for fifteen minutes. No, in the future, everyone will sit next to someone famous for at least fifteen minutes."

Movie critic Frank Schneck posits that the word should be film, not fame: "Andy Warhol was wrong. It's not just that everyone is going to have 15 minutes of fame. In the not-so-distant future, every person on the planet is going to have a film made about him or her" (*Hollywood Reporter*, 2000). Others seem to agree, in a roundabout way:

- "Andy Warhol was wrong. Today it seems that anyone can parlay their 15 minutes of fame into 15 cable episodes, with an option for a second season." —"It's Unreal How Easily Reality Shows Pop Up," *Rocky Mountain Daily News*, July 20, 2002
- "Andy Warhol was wrong. Everyone's not going to be famous for 15 minutes; instead, we will all have our own talk shows." —"Ex-Dancer, Ex-First Son Tries a New Career: Talk Show Host," *Buffalo News*, Aug. 16, 1991

Then there are those who argue that the 15 minutes are recurring:

- "The couple who wrote and performed the theme to the 1970s TV series "Happy Days" are on a media blitz in Colorado Springs this weekend, proving that Andy Warhol was wrong. Not only will everyone in the world get 15 minutes of fame, they'll get another 15 minutes when the nostalgia factor kicks in a couple of decades later." —"These Days Are Happy for Couple," *The Gazette*, March 6, 1997

- "Andy Warhol was wrong ... People don't want 15 minutes of fame in their lifetime. They want it every night." —"Pseudo's Josh Harris," *BusinessWeek*, Jan. 26, 2000
- "Andy Warhol was wrong. With the release of the film, Factory Girl, he and his 'superstars' are about to get another 15 minutes of fame." —"Straight to the Point," *Daily Mail*, Sept. 27, 2006
- "As it turns out, Andy Warhol was wrong: not everybody will be famous for 15 minutes. But with bad prospects and a good agent, those who once were can now extend the clock thanks to unprecedented TV demands for the vaguely familiar." —Vinay Menon, "More Dancing with Quasi-Celebs," *Toronto Star*, March 19, 2007

Not fame, but Hitler:

- "Andy Warhol was wrong. In the future, everyone will be Hitler for 15 minutes." —"Originality is the First Casualty of War," Austin American-Statesman, April 1, 1999
- "Andy Warhol got it wrong. It's not fame everyone will have in the future; It's a chance to scream at someone else on TV." —"Clinton Vs. Dole About Ratings, Not Discourse," *Witicha Eagle*, March 11, 2003

Not fame, but privacy:

- "Andy Warhol was wrong. The wild-eyed artist boldly proclaimed that in the future everyone would have 15 minutes of fame. Warhol's fortune-telling skills were nowhere as visionary as his art. Warhol should have predicted with the explosion of reality television that in the future everyone will have 15 minutes of privacy." —"One Day, We'll Beg for Privacy," *Fresno Bee*, Aug. 3, 2000

Not fame, but Colorado citizenship:
- "Andy Warhol was wrong. It turned out we were all from Colorado." —Barry Fagin, "Montel Williams and Me," *Independence Institute*, Nov. 1, 2000

Not fame, but hostage crisis:
- "In the future, everyone will be a hostage for fifteen minutes." —William Keckler

Fame, yes, but in the past, not in the future:
- "Andy Warhol was wrong. Everybody already has been famous--some time last week. It just depends on who's telling it and who's listening." —"The Remembering Game," *Depot Town Rag*, Sept. 1990

Fame, yes, but not 15 minutes exactly:
- "Andy Warhol got it wrong by 12 minutes. People have three minutes of fame; long enough to walk down a catwalk and back." —*Guardian*, July 7, 2002
- "Warhol was wrong ... cos he was 10 minutes off; it's really five minutes now." —"Meat Loaf Criticises Academic 'Laziness,'" TVNZ, March 9, 2010
- "The culture-shock doctor explained that science had discovered that Andy Warhol was wrong about fame; He had the right idea, but his figures were off." —"The Sting of Cable Backlash," *Miami Herald*, Oct. 9, 1983
- "'Andy Warhol was wrong,' Neal Gabler said. 'He was right when he said everyone will be famous, but wrong about the 15 minutes.'" —Marjorie Kaufman,

"Seeking the Roots of a Celebrity Society," *New York Times*, Dec. 11, 1994

Fame, yes, but for more like 15 seconds:

- "Andy Warhol was wrong. Everyone can be famous these days, all right, but the renown lasts more like 15 seconds, not minutes." —"Smile! You're Part of a Video Society," *Greensboro News and Record*, May 20, 1990
- "Andy Warhol was wrong when he said that everyone would have 15 minutes of fame; extras can look forward to having only seconds of movie glory." —"12 Hours' Extra Work for a Brief Moment of Glory," *Derby Evening Telegraph*, Nov. 9, 2006
- "[A cuckoo clock bird speaking:] Andy Warhol was wrong; I only get 15 seconds of fame." —Mike Peters, "Mother Goose and Grimm," July 27, 2005
- "Andy Warhol was wrong. In my case, at least, fame clocked in at only 6:42 minutes, and that was before the final cut." —Wilborn Hampton Lead, "Confessions of a Soap Opera Extra," *New York Times*, Dec. 31, 1989
- "Andy Warhol was wrong when he said that everyone will enjoy their fifteen minutes of fame. The time frame he referred to might one day be measured in seconds." —Warren Adler, "The Dividing Line," Aug. 10, 2009
- "Little did I realize that not only would there be no money, but that your star would flicker for two seconds and that was it." —Holly Woodlawn, quoted in her NYT obituary, Dec. 7, 2015

Fame, yes, but for more than 15 minutes:

- "Andy Warhol was wrong. You can be famous for a lot longer than 15 minutes, if you're clever enough." —"Oliver's Brand of Revitalisation," *Marketing Week*, April 7, 2005

- "'We were sure that Andy Warhol was wrong, that it would last more than 15 minutes,' says Hilary Jay." —"Maximal Art and Its Rise from the Ashes," *Philadelphia Inquirer*, July 25, 1993

- "When it comes to the Super Bowl, Andy Warhol was wrong. Its cast of characters has been famous for 25 years, and will be 25 years from now." —"Simply the Best," *Denver Post*, Jan. 27, 1991

- "Andy Warhol was wrong. Long after the buzzer sounded on Mark Fuhrman's 15 minutes of fame, he just won't go away." —"Fuhrman Overstaying His Welcome," June 10, 2001

- "Andy Warhol was wrong: sometimes you do get more than 15 minutes of fame, even if you're not Greg Louganis." —*National Review*, Dec. 10, 2004

- "Andy Warhol was wrong. Not everyone gets 15 minutes of fame. Many people get more than that. Like Dr. Bernie Dahl." —*The Nashua Telegraph*, Dec. 3, 2000

- "Andy Warhol was wrong. In the Ultimate universe we've got more than 15 minutes." —"Hack Meets Hacker," *Aspen Magazine*, Midsummer 1996

- "Andy Warhol was wrong ... you can have 45 minutes of fame, not just 15!" —"Invitation to Present at the OTM SIG Conference in June 2009," Dec. 22, 2008

- "Andy Warhol was wrong in my case; my fifteen minutes of fame have been more like three hours." —Ken Eichele, *My Best Day in Golf: Celebrity Stories of the Game They Love*, 2003

- "Andy Warhol was wrong; I was a hero for at least fifteen hours." —Gene GeRue, "Tomato Madness," Dec. 17, 2006

- "Andy Warhol was wrong. People aren't famous for fifteen minutes; they're famous forever." —Arthur Black, *Black & White and Read All Over*, 2004

Fame, yes, but "in" 15 minutes, not "for" 15 minutes:

- "Andy Warhol was wrong, when he predicted that in the future, people would become famous for 15 minutes. This is the future. Now people become famous in 15 minutes. Take Duran Duran." —Ethlie Ann Vare, "New Echoes of Duran Duran," *New York Times*, Nov. 24, 1985

Fame, yes, but without measure:

- "Andy Warhol was wrong. In the future, everyone will not be famous for 15 minutes. Everyone will just be famous." —"Cooking Up Celebrity Storm," *Boston Globe*, Jan. 21, 2000
- "Andy Warhol was wrong. No one is famous for just 15 minutes. These days you get to be famous whenever you feel like it. Just like everyone else." —"Now, Everyone is Famous! Who Knew?" *Associated Press*, July 16, 1999
- "'Andy Warhol was wrong,' says Newman, who completed his trek in 1987. 'If I wanted to be boring, I could live on this for the rest of my life." —"Book Lists Sometime-Dubious Firsts," *Dallas Morning News*, July 31, 1988
- "Andy Warhol was wrong about one thing: His own 'fifteen minutes of fame' have never ended." —B&N, review of *Andy Warhol Treasures*, 2009
- "In the internet age, bad headlines no longer go away and Andy Warhol was wrong about his fifteen minutes of fame. If you are infamous now, you are infamous forever." —Peter Walsh, "Curtis Warren: the Celebrity Drug Baron," *Telegraph*, Oct. 7, 2009

The opposite of fame:

- "Milwaukee futurist David Zach says Andy Warhol was wrong: We aren't going to get that 15 minutes

of fame after all. 'It's just the opposite,' Zach says."
—Tim Nelson, "The Skinny," *St. Paul Pioneer Press*,
Aug. 27, 1998

- "I think Andy Warhol got it wrong: in the future, so many people are going to become famous that one day everybody will end up being anonymous for 15 minutes." —Shepard Fairey, *Swindle #8*, 2006

- "Andy Warhol was wrong. Most of us will never come close to being famous—even for 15 minutes." —"Stepping into the Spotlight," *Wall Street Journal*, Nov. 8, 1999

Fifteen, yes, but not minutes:

- "Andy Warhol was wrong: not everyone deserves 15 minutes of fame. Some people deserve 160 words of recognition ..." —"Unsung Heroes," *What Magazine*, Jan. 1, 2004

- "Andy Warhol was wrong: for 15 minutes, everybody gets to be a starting quarterback for The Saints." —"Tyson Still Has Issues," *Atlanta Journal*, Oct. 16, 1998

- "Andy Warhol was wrong: in the future, everyone won't be famous for 15 minutes, but everyone will have their own Web site." —"Book Review: The Non-Designer's Web Book," *Information Management Journal*, July 1, 1999

- "Andy Warhol was wrong. We've all had our 15 minutes, now we all want a mini-series!" —"Boy First Believed On Runaway Balloon Found After Frantic Search," *New York Post*, Oct. 16, 2009

- "Andy Warhol was wrong. Everyone won't just have 15 minutes of fame. One day—soon, I suspect—we all will have our very own talk shows." —Linda L.S. Schulte, "Word's Worth," *Baltimore Sun*, Jan. 31, 1996

- "In the future, we'll all have 15 minutes of future." —*Nein Quarterly*

- "In the future, everyone will be offended for 15 years." —Sean Tejaratchi

Fame, yes, but perhaps 30 minutes:

- "There are times in life when you just hope that Andy Warhol was wrong and that a merciful God will grant you a second 15 minutes of fame." —"Confessions of an Embarrassed Viagra Expert," *University Wire*, Sept. 24, 1998

Just plain wrong:

- "The endless parade of disposable rock bands, special-effects movies, potboiler thriller novels and TV sitcoms makes me think that Andy Warhol was wrong." —"Longtime Newsweek Art Critic Peter Plagens is Also a Painter," *Newsweek*, April 25, 2002
- "A TV producer played by Joe Mantegna muses that Andy Warhol was wrong about everybody being famous for 15 minutes." —"Allen's 'Celebrity' Witty, Wicked But Shallow," *Wichita Eagle*, Dec. 9, 1998
- "Andy Warhol was wrong - everyone does NOT have their 15 minutes of fame and the overwhelming majority of You're a Star hopefuls would have told him that." —"The Fame Game's Just Not Worth It," *The Mirror*, Aug. 25, 2006
- "Andy Warhol was wrong. When you're a Vanderbilt running back, you're not famous for 15 minutes." —A. Lane, *Nashville City Paper*, Nov. 5, 2004
- "My main conclusion: Andy Warhol was wrong— we won't all get 15 minutes of fame." —"Using the Internet to Examine Patterns of Foreign Coverage," *Nieman Reports*, Sept. 22, 2004
- "Warhol was wrong. The message is clear: we do not want your 15 minutes of fame, you can shove it." —Alix Sharkey, "Saturday Night: The Techno Ice-Cream Van is on its Way," *The Independent*, June

26, 1993
- "Warhol was wrong! He neglected to factor in the 15 minutes of one's own alter-egos." —"Warhol was Wrong," GenderFun.com, May 29, 2009

Life begins after ...

- death
- coffee
- sunset
- a reset
- puberty
- analysis
- midnight
- retirement
- five o'clock
- high school
- you get fired
- you say "I do"
- business hours
- the question mark
- the transfiguration
- the day of judgement
- weapons are returned
- the introductory chapters
- one's second cup of coffee
- putting your house in order
- spending days lying under a pear tree
- one enters a state of superconsciousness

What sustains us is...

- telling stories
- an irrational hope
- apples, the season's last tomatoes, a sprinkle of snow
- outrageous aspirations
- our faith in the final rightness of things
- that we're not traveling alone
- ideological firmness
- the act of kindness
- the empty landscape
- when we find a way to be compassionate
- greater than we are and beyond our control
- prayer
- not something ordinary
- our culture
- the dark energy to which we go periodically to be renewed
- what precedes us
- a form of realization of what it is we already are
- a sense that there is a promised land
- the primal temple
- the consciousness that, after all, we are right, and that though things may move slowly, yet the end is sure
- everywhere and in everything—or it's nowhere at all

A baker's dozen of things that inspire "wordless awe"

- the star-encrusted heavens
- the thunderous silence of Yosemite
- a classically beautiful woman
- a diamond necklace
- cherry blossoms
- nature's grandeur
- anatomical knowledge
- standing atop Mt. Wilson
- the thought of God
- scientific discoveries
- the shrouded dead
- new life
- ancient architectural wonders

A dozen things talking skulls have said

- "There is no use for you to cry, for you are with me now, and you must begin to clean me." —told by storyteller White Sun, whose grandfather was the medicine-man of the Kitkehahki (*The Pawnee Mythology*, collected by George Dorsey, 1906).

- "Is it just today or yesterday that I have been here?" —a Nigerian Yoruba story (*African Folktales in the New World* by William Bascom, 1992).

- "I was dreaming. ...I dreamt that I threw my own body down. I dreamt that I was bounding about, merely a skull." —*Yana Texts* by Edward Sapir, 1910

- "There is as much fire beneath our feet and heads as the sky is distant from the earth." —*The Book of the Elders: Sayings of the Desert Fathers*, translated by John Wortley, 2012

- "Shall I remain a skull for ever, or shall I take my own true form?" —"*The Two Sisters,*" *A Staircase of Stories* chosen by Louey Chisholm and Amy Steedman, 1920

- "Why do you spurn me? I once was living, I now am rolling in the dust; your fate will be like mine." — *Smoke* by Ivan Sergeevich Turgenev, 1883

- "Tongue brought me here; tongue will bring you here too." —*Readers of the Quilt* by Joanne Dowdy, 2005

- "I have fully enjoyed valuable treasures in my life time—and even after I died." —*Uighur Stories from Along the Silk Road*, 1998

- The skull spoke. Muffled. Sepulchral. "Trick or treat!" —*Hunter's Orange* by William Dieter, 1984

- "Foolishness killed me, and cleverness has killed you." —*Research in African Literatures*, 1977

- "We ask you to look with the eyes of your soul and to engage with the essential. Regaining your luminous nature is a possibility today for all who dare to take the leap." —*The Maya End Times* by Patricia Mercier, 2008

- "I am here to destroy all human beings." —*Curse of the Crystal Skull* by Drac Von Stoller, 2012

The only decision is ...

- where to place everything
- whether to do this in orbit or on the ground
- which is the lesser evil
- between the arduous and the incoherent
- which shredder to use
- whether to release the tie-backs and let the curtains hide you
- to launch or to forego the mission
- whether or not to play
- to believe or not to believe that the apparatus and its operator are trustworthy
- between down and up
- whether or not the drug should be used at all
- when to reschedule
- between the second and third options
- where to start
- to determine how private the conversation is
- how to present it
- whether to cross the room and take a handful
- between cooperation and aloofness
- whether to report zero or one
- to strange or smother
- choosing between all-chocolate and all-vanilla
- whether to send an individual or a committee
- do you squeeze or pour?
- whether to accept or reject suggested numbers
- which bad guy to take out next

- whether or not to add water
- to leave frustrated or attack
- whether you want to live or not
- which door to enter
- whether there is anything to be gained
- one of signal direction
- whether we are at inflow or outflow point
- the right decision

Clouds want many things:

- The clouds want to know what they are. (*The Journal of the Anthropological Society of Bombay*, 1928)
- The clouds want to be your clothes. (Shidao Xu, *Origins of Chinese Cuisine*, 2003)
- The clouds want more elaboration. (Horatio Noble Pym, *Odds and Ends at Foxwold*, 1887)
- The clouds want to hide the sun. (Don Marion Wolfe, *Language Arts and Life Patterns*, 1972)
- The clouds want to rain on the parade; they have intentionality. (Jonathan C. Smith, *Pseudoscience and Extraordinary Claims of the Paranormal*, 2011)
- Clouds want to be fields. (Nichita Stanescu, *Wheel with a Single Spoke: and Other Poems*, 2012)
- The clouds want to play. (Kevin R. Fish, *Poetic Justice For Nature*, 2004)
- In general, clouds want a full baptism in the sea. (Gaius Glenn Atkins, *The Godward Side of Life*, 1917)
- The clouds want to go somewhere. (David Hicks, *Ritual and Belief: Readings in the Anthropology of Religion*, 2010)
- Clouds want to be platforms. (Curtis Franklin Jr., *Cloud Computing: Technologies and Strategies of the Ubiquitous Data Center*, 2009)
- Fragments of clouds want to align. (Paul S. Ropp, *Banished Immortal*, 2002)
- Clouds want to move things around, get a better view where noise comes from. (Devan Malore, *The Churning*, 2008)
- Our clouds want to mingle and form an even bigger and better cloud. (Sol Gordon, *How Can You Tell If You're Really In Love?*, 2001)

- Clouds want to blow in and drop rain. (Marianne Sawicki, *Crossing Galilee*, 2000)
- Clouds want more moisture in order to remain supportive. (Ham Kaima, *My Arrogant Friends*, 1992)
- The clouds want to be smoke circles blown over lips. (A. Van Jordan, *Quantum Lyrics: Poems*, 2007)
- Hovering dark clouds want to flatten the city. (*Chinese Idioms and Phrases*, 1977)
- The clouds want fire from the rocks. (Courtenay Malcolm Batchelor, *Folklore*, 1952)
- All clouds want a talent. (Dow Kump, *Scooter's Sparking Stone*, 2005)

Comedy is "at risk." And that would be funny if it weren't so ...

- serious
- unwittingly ironic
- provoking
- stupid
- pathetic
- prevalent
- frustrating
- tragic
- dangerously misinformed
- terrifying
- sad
- pitiful
- ludicrous
- destructive
- impressive
- gross
- scary
- true
- disastrous
- disgusting
- painful
- probable
- terrible
- patently ridiculous
- sincere

- perverse
- unfunny
- horrible
- stressful
- outrageous
- ill-bred
- sickening
- insulting
- crazy
- typical
- deadly
- insidious
- grotesque
- significant
- absurd
- real
- despicable
- wicked
- bitter
- wide of the mark
- common
- moralizing
- filled with pathos
- vile
- cruel
- appalling
- hideous
- painfully revealing
- very nearly unbearable

- important
- predictable
- expensive
- heartbreaking
- damn personal

There's no time for ...

- dillydallying
- crying
- changing your mind
- waiting
- chit-chat
- repentance
- deliberation
- grudges
- hesitation
- subtleties
- fussing and fighting
- cuckoo clocks
- extracurricular activities
- diplomacy
- flourishes
- buts
- do-overs
- sorrow
- feelings
- slumber
- dessert
- goldbricking
- idle brooding
- civility
- pity
- distractions
- daydreaming

- second chances
- feeling sorry
- cuddling
- the news
- grand exits

If everybody would just ...

- mind their own business
- lighten up a little
- lay their cards on the table
- get organized
- decide what they want
- sit down in a circle
- look at the positive
- plant a little patch
- love and respect each other
- do their share
- stop judging
- obey the Golden Rule
- pull together
- eat an apple a day
- begin picking up after themselves
- behave as we do
- tell the truth
- take a breather
- play and stop yelling
- listen
- hang on
- pass their wallets around
- lend a hand occasionally
- concentrate on their personal strengths
- play it safe
- be patient
- be fair

- treat others as they would be treated
- promise not to do it again
- shut up for ten days in a row
- leave me alone
- stop trying so hard
- be frank and sincere
- stop getting in the way
- learn the basic rules of conduct for life
- relax and let me do it

We should immediately ...

- cover ourselves in camouflage nets
- apply a dozen or more leeches
- take action to undo the contorted posture of inaction into which we have been twisted by events of the past few years
- bring forth a mind of respect
- confess our faults
- pull back our forces
- think of the Buddha's name
- establish a modern communication policy
- recall the faults of anger
- get a truer glimpse of the inner struggles
- set up a complete blockade
- reduce our unnecessarily large consumption of butter and condensed milk
- engage in prayer
- stress that there is no better fuel than uncertainty to promote speculation
- end the chaos
- create a file folder
- consult with our allies
- tune the transmitter to that frequency and answer when the calling station gives the invitation
- change the basic equations of both kinematics and dynamics
- extricate ourselves
- recognize the necessity of making plain the ambiguity of the terms as the very first step in our explanation

Good cheer is made expressly for ...

- dark days
- disappointments
- dubious faces
- cross-patches
- sick-rooms
- bitter medicines
- bad news
- anger clouds
- hard lessons
- failures
- blues
- all croakers

—*Alys-All-Alone* by Una Macdonald, 1911

Going beyond *The Importance of Being Earnest:*

THE IMPORTANCE OF BEING STERNEST

THE IMPORTANCE of BEING FURNISHED

THE IMPORTANCE OF BEING BURNISHED

THE IMPORTANCE OF BEING FURTHEST

The Importance of Being Curtis

importance of being purposed

the importance of being Kurdish

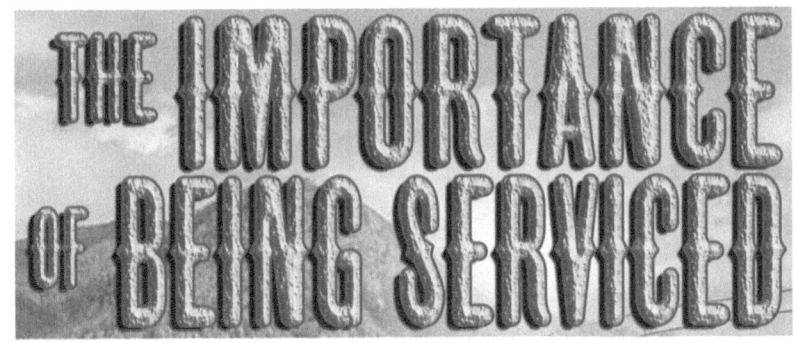

"The Importance of Being Turnips."

The Impotence of Being Earnest

The Importance of Beating Earnest

the importance of earnest 'being'.

The Earnest Being of Importance

THE EARNESTNESS OF BEING IMPORTANT

Part Two

Lists of a different nature
(Non-ironic and/or non-collaged from disparate sources)

People's 13 top fears about numerology

- What if I'm a zero?
- What if I'm only a fraction of who I thought I was?
- What if I'm odd?
- What if 13 isn't unlucky and all the ways I've structured my life around superstition have been in vain?
- Decimalization.
- What if I'm tested on the difference between numbers and numerals?
- What if I turn out to be negative, like I've occasionally be accused of being.
- What if I can't do the math?
- What if all I'm left with is a "remainder"?
- What if I confuse infinite decimals with infinitesimals?
- What if someone tries to "high five" me?
- What if I turn out to be irrational?
- What if calculators aren't allowed?
- What if all that separates math from myth is a y?
- What if it's considered cheating to employ *Astronumerography*?

Items in an old list, in my own handwriting, that I have absolutely no memory of

- Hiccup cures
- Lessons to be learned from rest[aurant] servers
- How to spot a threatening cloud
- Deeper meaning of bad dreams
- Building materials that can fit in your pocket
- Books that offer a good explanation of things
- Haikus

In a 1939 volume of *Daily Tar Heel,* there are references to...

- pink elephants
- golden fleece
- ghost writing
- cindermen
- phantoms
- mermen
- wolfmen
- wolves
- devils
- grail
- imps

Sublime colors are commonly described as being...

- incomparably beautiful
- exquisite
- cheerful
- timeless
- soft
- active
- natural (sunrise, clouds, rainbows, mountains, or sea, for example)
- radiant
- sentimental
- magnificent
- glorious
- lofty, divine (in that they foster a spiritual experience)
- shimmering

Finally, a set of hourglasses for every occasion, including...

- the 1 minute manager
- the 2 minute warning
- the 3 minute egg
- the 4 minute mile
- the 5 minute break
- the 6 minute walk test
- the 7 minute difference
- the 8 minute epic
- the 9 minute chariot race

White horses appear in the religious literature of many lands. Here's a small sampling

- In the New Testament's Book of Revelation, one of the four horsemen of the Apocalypse rides a white horse.
- In Japan, the white horse is a Shinto symbol of purity and divine authority.
- In Islam, the Prophet ascended to heaven on the back of a white horse.
- In Hinduism, the god Kalki rides a white horse while brandishing a comet-like sword.
- In Nordic lore, the god Odin rises a white horse named Sleipnir.
- In Greek mythology, the white and winged Pegasus sprang from the blood of Medusa when Perseus decapitated her.

There are many "evil trinities," including...

- treachery, cruelty, and superstition (the evil trinity of the Spaniard, in *Sir Ferdinando Gorges and His Province of Maine* by James Phinney Baxter, 1890)
- alcohol, ignorance, and immorality (the evil trinity of backwoods settlements, in *Colliers*, 1915)
- cowardice, impatience, and self-love (the evil trinity of a fatal course, in *Bonnie Kate* by Mrs. De Courcy Laffan, 1894)
- lice, impure food, and foul water (the "evil trinity of chicken raising," in *American Poultry Advocate*, 1914)
- lust of the flesh, lust of the eye, and pride of life (the evil trinity of corruption, in *The American National Preacher*, 1843)
- servitude, destitition, and ignorance (the "evil trinity of political debasement," in *Eagle Pass* by Cora Montgomery, 1852)
- the boss, the speculator, and the soulless corporation (the evil trinity of public park sanitation, in *Popular Science Monthly*, 1899)
- appetite in the drunkard, greed in the liquor maker and seller, and indifference in church members (the evil trinity of temperance work, in *Minutes of the General Assembly of the Presbyterian Church in the United States*, 1892)
- the world, the flesh, and the Devil (the evil trinity of the soul's enemies in Christian theology)
- infidelity, anti-Christianity, and Spiritism (the evil trinity of unclean spirits in *American Messianic Fellowship Monthly*, 1917)
- ignorance, superstition, and prejudice (the evil trinity that plots human misery, in *The School News and Practical Educator*, 1904)

The lovely song "Autumn's Edge" by Xeno & Oaklander got us wondering what else happens at autumn's edge. Here's what we discovered in the literature:

At autumn's edge...

- you bear a progeny of dust for nine months (Ricardo Pau-Llosa)
- leaves are still green yet curled and tired (Alastair Macdonald)
- we are unaware of the most significant moments (Linda Faltin)
- is a broken stretch of tussocky grass (Tom Pow)
- dreams slow to the bell and sheep cold-nibble the sun (Walter E. Kidd)
- the hunter time looms (*Ironwood*)
- old lord winter waits (*Triskell Tales*)
- a flaming pen comes into view (*The Improvement Era*)
- literary people are waiting for payment (So Chongju)

A poet's most recent web searches

- "recreational activities of unicorns"
- "People who have been killed by rainbows"
- "If you drop a multivitamin on the floor and can't find it, can a superpowerful insect develop?"
- "the lifespan of a clipped toenail" (again lost on the floor, presumably to be used as a weapon by the vitamined-up bug)
- "animals and insects that resemble Lady Gaga"
- "has anyone been charged with date raping himself or herself"
- "did Buddha have a masseur or masseuse?"
- "erotic attraction to snowmen or snowwomen"
- "who invented the snowbunny"
- "how common was cursing among caveman"
- "numbers between 0 and 9 which have been forgotten"
- "the longest recorded 'sorry, wrong number' conversation in history"
- "stalked and killed for dialing a wrong number"
- "the i.q. of dust bunnies"
- "people who disappeared attempting time travel"
- "people who wrote love letters to popes"
- "the funniest cartoon by a caveman discovered"
- "who made the first ass xerox?"
- "annotated history of the snowbunny"
- "fear of alphabetical order"

A phosphene is a multicolored shape or pattern seen in the darkness, without external visual stimulation. Phosphenes can be seen with closed eyes or in a completely dark room with open eyes.

Phosphenes may appear as...

- spirals
- exploding stars
- wispy clouds
- wheels
- tunnels
- parallel lines
- wavy lines
- dotted lines
- zigzags
- checkerboards
- honeycombs
- spider webs
- dot patterns
- circles within circles
- crosses
- thin meandering lines, like lightning
- geometric shapes, like triangles, squares, pentagons
- and so on.

Phosphenes can also be seen under such conditions as…

- hypnosis
- reverie
- fever delirium
- fatigue
- sensory deprivation
- sweat lodges
- profound concentration
- hyperventilation
- medicinal herbs
- psychoactive drugs (such as LSD)
- food and water deprivation
- electrical and magnetic stimulation of the visual cortex
- strobe lights
- rhythmic movement
- migraine headaches
- meditation
- trance states
- intense emotion
- stress
- crystal gazing

According to my research in *A Field Guide to Identifying Unicorns by Sound* . . .

The captivating, lightsome voice of a unicorn may sound like . . .

- a wondrous cascading
- an exotic lullaby
- something out of a fairy tale
- a strange, melodic chuckling
- a trickling flute
- a comfort
- a mourning dove
- an angelic shower
- a happy cooing
- Ella Fitzgerald
- spiritually-charged vibrations
- burbling water
- something from the future
- peculiarly clear

Some favorite words from the lyrics of the Swedish band Bodies without Organs

- juggernaut
- thunderdome
- transhuman
- electrolyte
- halcyon
- bourgeoise
- tarmac
- mundane
- odyssey
- expressway
- cobblestones
- favela
- consecrating
- galvanized
- supersonic
- masquerade
- Martian invasion
- testosterone
- supernova
- boogaloo
- Himalayas

Why unicorns and snowflakes are so similar

- no two alike
- sparkly white in color (having absorbed all of the surrounding sunlight or moonlight)
- difficult to predict
- beautiful
- symbols of purity
- natural materializations
- symbols of innocence
- can be dangerous at times
- symbols of serenity
- excellent insulators
- ephemeral
- blend into the landscape

From *A Field Guide to Identifying Unicorns by Sound.*

We once tried to buy a photograph of Woody Allen. We called the photographer to ask about availability, and he laughed at us. "That's not Woody Allen," he explained condescendingly. "That's a wax figure of Woody Allen." Then he began hemming and hawing, talking about how much trouble it would be to find the negative and make a print. (Artists, bless 'em, can be real pieces of work themselves.) Flustered by the entire conversation, we politely told him not to put himself out and decided not to pursue the acquisition. But here's the lingering question: had the photo been of Woody Allen himself and not an uncannily lifelike wax figure, might we have worked past the photographer's primadonna attitude and secured a print? I mean, we loved the photo, but did it feel somehow less authentic in its waxy afterglow?

Here's what we do know about wax figures

- "Every day a wax figure is taken for a live man, and live people are mistaken for wax." —Richard Panchyk, *New York City History for Kids*, 2012
- "The complexion of a wax figure is indeed a work of art." —*American Cloak and Suit Review*, 1918
- "A wax figure is not cheap, especially a good one." —*Dry Goods Reporter*, 1906
- "A wax figure is a material thing." —L. W. Forguson, "Has Ayer Vindicated the Sense-Datum Theory?"
- "A wax figure is understood by us as something constructed by an intelligent mind." —Jehangir Nasserwanji Chubb, *Faith Possesses Understanding*, 1983

And yet:

- "A wax figure is repulsive; it is stiff and stark and reminds us of a corpse." —Schopenhauer, "The Metaphsics of Fine Art," *Religion: A Dialogue, and Other Essays*, 1891

Some things that sound funnier than they are

- amusia — a less-than amusing condition in which one loses musical ability. (Erin McKean's *Weird and Wonderful Words*.)
- the zany plots of most ghost comedies. (*The TV Times Film and Video Guide*.)
- Montezuma's Revenge. (Florence Crannell Means' *Emmy and the Blue Door*.)
- a "tepid boxoffice blunder." (*Videohound's Golden Movie Retriever*.)
- a penile Swiss Army knife bristling with attachments. (*Hollywood East: Hong Kong Movies and the People Who Made Them*.)
- last rites spoken in Pig Latin. ("Pluck You, Too!" blog.)
- sexsomnia — unwanted "sleep sex." (News producer Stephanie Smith.)
- snoring
- cuckolding
- a mounted Boer. (*The Bedside 'Guardian,'* Vol. 23.)
- a 6-foot tall rabbit called Frank. (*Donnie Darko*.)

How to tell the difference between actors John Hurt and John Heard

John Hurt was hurting when:

- an alien burst through his chest in *Alien*
- he was taken to the dreaded "Room 101" in *1984*
- Sir Thomas More wouldn't give him a job in *A Man for All Seasons*
- when his elephantitis was exploited in *The Elephant Man*

John Heard was a good listener when:

- his lover turned into a roaring leopard in *Cat People*
- a guy in his bar was just trying to get back home in *After Hours*
- he learned about the interdependence of all systems in *Mindwalk*
- when his family adopted a wayward girl in *Rambling Rose*

"There ain't a lighter hand at a pudden, though I say that shouldn't." From *Lettice Lisle* by Lady Verney, 1870. So...

The lighter the hand, the lighter the pudding. But also:

- "The more devastating the criticism, the lighter the hand has to be." (Lester B. Lave, quoted in "A Life that Mattered")
- "The lighter the hand, the more berries in the pan." (*Fedco Seeds*)
- "The lighter the hand, the lighter the biscuit." (*Convivial*)
- "The lighter the hand of the sawyer, the better the saw operates." (Luke Miner, "Sawing Lessons: Kierkegaard's Concluding Unscientific Postcript")
- "The lighter the hand, the flakier the crust." (Food Network)
- "The lighter the hand of the [tattoo] artist on the needle, the less pain you'll have during the procedure." (Beth Asaff, "Pain of Getting a Tattoo in Different Places")
- "When applying a concealing makeup, the lighter the hand, the better." (The Sturge-Weber Foundation)
- "The lighter the hand of the guiding adult, the more motivated and spontaneous the play is likely to be." (Anne Burke, *Ready to Learn: Using Play to Build Literacy Skills in Young Learners*)
- "The lighter the hand, the closer you can wear [perfume] to your nose." (Perfume Interview with Judith of Unseen Censer, Part I)
- "For the lighter the hand becomes, the deeper you will go." (Marjor Mark Cunningham, "Intro to Hypnosis")

Attending a Mime's Birthday Party: The Do's and Don'ts

As we all know, mimes deal only with invisible boxes. If you wish to give a mime a birthday present, it must be enclosed in a transparent box or bag. Finding a clear wrapping isn't too much of a challenge. But what can you put in that clear wrapping that won't immediately spoil the surprise? Actually, the sky's the limit! Here are some clear winners:

- a set of shot glasses
- a crystal ball
- a transparent novelty toilet seat
- a clear quartz pendant
- a beveled glass suncatcher
- translucent sandals
- a clear vinyl shower curtain
- a clear rain poncho
- a set of empty CD cases
- bottled water
- a clear glass paperweight
- plastic wrap
- acrylic martini glasses
- a crystal clear iPOD NANO case
- a pressed glass serving platter
- a cut lead crystal flower vase
- a window pane
- a clear plastic comb
- an invisible painting
- a lucite and mirror coffee table

Now for the Don'ts:
- When visiting a mime's house, don't throw stones.

Some uncommon wisdom from unlikely sources

- Never go with a hippie to a second location. (*30 Rock*, NBC series)
- Never drink with a savage. (*The Western Lands* by William Burroughs)
- The best way to avoid a confrontation with a stranger: never walk through a strange neighborhood. (Maharishi Mahesh Yogi)
- Nothing is better calculated to antagonize the wealthy than to ask for a small loan. (*The Western Lands* by William Burroughs)
- There is no cure for injustice other than committing another injustice to correct the first—let the river wash away the bad blood. (*Ancient Evenings* by Norman Mailer)

The great Australian comedy series *Kath & Kim* features some...

Hilariously dumbfounding baby names

- Typhphaanniii (pronounced Tiffany)
- Eppinn'knee Rae¨</i> (Rae is followed by an [umlaut] and a [close italics])
- Detestannii
- Paloma
- Papiloma
- Tailuh (pronounced Tai Luh)
- Glen Waverley (after a suburb in Victoria, Australia)
- Aussie
- Fat Free Frûche
- Tiramisu

Then there are these baby names, inspired by a hospital visit (and please note that they all sound better with an Australian accent):

- Neil Bymouth
- Cardio Infarction (the downside being the inevitable nickname "Farct")
- Enema (for a girl)
- Lupus (for a boy)
- Catheter
- I.V. (for a girl)

Modeling One's Life After *Dark Shadows*: Studiedly Stoddard

Tips on how to conduct oneself, based upon the character of Elizabeth Collins Stoddard:

- Always look your best, even if your husband isn't buried in the basement.
- Plant your feet firm on the deck when a gale blows. Hold your head up high and damn the devil, because you don't know how to run scared.
- To clarify what you have heard and slow down the episodes of your life, repeat the last word spoken by whomever is talking to you. For example: "How are you today?" "Today?"
- Do your hair very high, and add a bow most of the time.
- Say you don't care about money, but if anyone tries to take yours, hit him in the head with a poker.
- Your makeup matters, even if your wrinkled lips smear the lipstick. It will matter more once you go to color.
- Hold back your tears. Choke back your emotion. Crying reveals your weakness, and no head of a cannery can afford emotion. Think of the dead fish you have to put out of your mind every day. If overwhelmed by feeling, let one or two tears escape, and dab them away delicately with a lace hanky. Loud sobbing is okay if alone in your room late at night, or when in the locked basement room.
- Write your death date in the family Bible in pencil or erasable ink. You never know, do you?
- Almost always, face the open window, your back to the guest, assuring fresh air.

- Wear a tasteful suit or dress, though you will not go out. You never know who will need to speak to you in the drawing room.
- Practice social distancing: work from home, limit guests to two at a time, and isolate them in the drawing room.
- Always add the family jewels. Pearls or a brooch, or both. Think Queen Elizabeth without the purse.
- Speaking to people, always say, "I need to speak with you." This sets them on edge, giving you an advantage as they contemplate the cause of your need. Then, ask them to step into the drawing room. Close the doors. You have thus taken command of both space and time and lent importance to even the simplest statement. Then say, "Thank you, but I don't wish to discuss it." They are completely at your mercy, having no idea what just happened.
- Always maintain that your marriage was one of the worst mistakes in your life.
- The cue you're looking for may be outside the drawing room window.
- Keep yourself separate from the town. Class distinctions are important. Granted, the occasional trip to the jail to bail out your daughter will be required, but never, ever, enter The Blue Whale. The dancing is atrocious.
- Try to read only family genealogy, the occasional magazine, or newspaper headlines (but only when a close friend has disappeared).
- It helps to have a narrator summarize your day as you begin each new one. It cuts through a lot of doubt as to what happened yesterday. And a diary takes a lot of time. Be aware that the narrator may change, affecting your day.

- Never hand over the key you keep on a chain around your neck.
- Prohibit anyone from loitering near the locked room in the basement.
- Secure some lacy bed jackets. A full robe is so cumbersome when you are being served tea in bed.
- Plan for a bell to be installed in your mausoleum just in case you're buried alive.
- Always avoid the question.
- Decline sherry if it is offered, unless it is the only thing to keep you from fainting.
- There is dignity in defending one's house guests to the death.
- Allow only one person to informally call you 'Liz.' That is Roger, your brother, but even he should reserve such casual address for the most intimate situations. Only answer to Mrs. Stoddard. Even to yourself.
- Be tortured by the presence of death. Others can't see it, of course, but if they look into your eyes, they'll know that you, somehow, can see it.
- Stay fit by strolling to Widow's Walk. Do not go there if you are feeling dizzy.
- When you don't know what to say, scan the room for a prompt. It gives you a desperate look and buys time for your response.
- Remind younger siblings and staff that you are the matriarch. Collinwood (or your address) belongs to you. You are in control until little David (or your own male heir) comes of age.
- Hands should be kept at your center, lightly clasped, or folded. This communicates your resolve to take no action of any kind in any situation. Neutrality and inaction equal power and class.

- Limit phones in the house to two. Place them within feet of each other. No need to take calls when you are trying to rest. The ghostly widows calling you to your death are enough disturbance at night.
- If you don't want people to know you are menopausal, avoid opening and closing windows during storms and while there is a fire in the fireplace. It's a dead giveaway you are having hot flashes.
- Most importantly, whatever it is, don't talk about it. Especially not over the phone. Or if it's late. But it you must, always go into the drawing room and close the doors. For God's sake, not the hall!

An old handwritten list, the meanings forgotten

- Jupiter
- Mars
- she
- I'm not in my body
- milkshake
- abstract
- yes/no
- Hawaii
- any vague sexual reference
- Mastercard/Visa
- chap
- anti-intellectualism
- poisonous food
- doctor's bills
- IGNORANCE is too harsh
- G.O.D.
- mush in people's mouths
- any playfulness
- Indian accent jokes
- tennis ball
- no clothes
- Chinese restaurant
- greediness
- silence
- carried list in wallet
- screaming into pillow

I've been compiling a list of things I excitedly told my kid brother 34 years ago, which he (annoyingly) scoffed at. These were ideas (from any number of sources) that captured my imagination but which irritated my brother's skeptical brain and stimulated his argumentative nature.

Ideas scoffed at

- Had dinosaurs not died out, they would have evolved into human beings. [I had seen a computer model proving this one, with an illustration of what a dino-human would have looked like (scaly skin, lizard-like features, human frame). In fairness to me, this was long, long before the general public had any reason to doubt computer models. So-called evidence aside, I'd say my brother's suspicions about this one were overly exaggerated.]

- The Navy cannot train dolphins to plant underwater bombs, because dolphins are pacifists. [I still like the idea of dolphins being pacifists. I heard this one from my professor of transformational/generative grammar. He didn't have the Navy's unclassified reports on hand.]

- Eskimos have hundreds of words for "snow," proving that different cultures experience different realities. [This is indeed an urban legend. My brother was right, though not necessarily for the right reasons.]

- The only reason dolphins don't paint, sculpt, play instruments, and build buildings is that they don't have hands. [In other words, dolphins don't have a culture due to a physical handicap, not because they're otherwise unevolved. I still like this idea.]

Arrested Development as the World's Grandest Aristocrats Joke

The vaudevillian dirty joke to end all dirty jokes, "The Aristocrats," is rarely told the same way twice, but it invariably transgresses unmentionable taboos with graphic oomph. The comedy series *Arrested Development* (Fox Broadcasting, 2003-2006) is a single, marvelously elaborate Aristocrats joke told over the course of 53 episodes. There's no way to overstate the degree of depravity on display. Granted, the scatology angle is subtly communicated (the plumbing of the family residence isn't hooked up to any sewer system, so the collective waste matter pools underneath until the structure and its residents begin to collapse into their own filth). But by no means subtle is the dizzyingly rampant incest between cousins, brothers, brothers and sisters, mothers and sons, fathers and sons, uncles and nephews, aunts and nephews, uncles and nieces—flavored with date rape drugs, disguises and costumes, cross-dressing, prosthetics, bananas, and robots to keep things spicy.

The classic Aristocrats joke begins with a fiercely immoral family visiting a talent agent, and we see this agent in the final episode of Arrested Development, in the person of series producer Ron Howard. This inversion is fitting, as each new Aristocrats joke is meant to turn its predecessors on their heads.

And so:

- Did you hear the one about the wealthy clan whose motto is "Family first?" (Ep. 1)
- Where exactly to begin? With the daughter sitting atop a copy machine at an office celebration and

handing her brother a photocopy of her vulva? (Ep. 41) With the mother giving her youngest son a camcorder so that he can videotape himself participating in a "naked pyramid" with his fellow Army recruits? (Ep. 25) With the twin brother's "only remaining pair of pants" blowing apart? (Ep. 39) Or with the eldest son using ether to knock out his father, then employing ventriloquism to make the unconscious man ask for a kiss and following through on the request? (Ep. 40)

- Revealingly, when the father describes "the sexiest creature I have ever laid eyes on," the middle son thinks it's about himself as he anticipates being made "his father's partner." (Ep. 1)

- In the crowded family car, the son-in-law notes that they're "ass to ankles" and asks his daughter to sit on her cousin's lap as the middle son cautions, "Bumpy road ahead!" Later, the middle son instructs his own son: "You're taking your cousin to work today . . . You stay on top of her, buddy; do not be afraid to ride her—hard." (Ep. 2) That's after the eldest son has discussed erections with his 13-year-old nephew, even as the daughter campaigns against circumcision and "saves enough skin to make ten new boys." (Ep. 1)

- The son-in-law searches through his wife's clothes for an outfit to wear to a family function, settling on a frilly blouse. (Ep. 1) But that's nothing—the extraordinary cross-dressing is yet to come. At one point he buys a fetish outfit when he thinks his daughter is into leather. (Ep. 9) And who could forget the time he joins the family for breakfast stark naked? (Ep. 13)

- Let's jump to the grandson and his cousin kissing on the lips for the benefit of his aunt. The fact that they're cousins is "what makes it funny." Later, they're tempted to kiss again in front of the entire family to "freak them out," and though it doesn't make sense, "isn't that what makes it funny?" (Ep. 1) This is before the boy is titillated by the trailer for "Dangerous Cousins" and tells his cousin, "We have got to see this movie." (Ep. 8) The boy compliments his cousin: "You're like this flower. And I know it's springtime, but I'd hate to see you get plucked by someone who doesn't even care that you're blossoming." (Ep. 39)

- For the entertainment of Alzheimer's patients, the grandson and his cousin participate in a purportedly mock wedding conducted by a real chaplain who proclaims, "Now they are truly family." Later, in a secret room in the house where the father keeps his gay porn magazines, the granddaughter expresses concern that it's wrong for cousins to marry. The grandson replies, "The Torah tells us that the larger wrong is to put our own feelings before the commitments we've made.... I'm not saying it's not weird for me too; I'm just saying maybe we could take those weird feelings and turn them into something positive." She considers, "I guess it would be a good way to freak out our parents..." "Let's freak them out!" (Ep. 50)

- Now things really heat up, as the two cousins are subsequently assigned the same bedroom. (Ep. 1) "Cousins can bunk together; that's why they call it bunkin' cousins." Later, the daughter separates the cousins, explaining to her nephew, "We're all just gonna have a more normal arrangement: I'm going to sleep with my daughter, and you're going to sleep with my husband." (Ep. 12) Her husband disrobes before his nephew to help banish the boy's seeming fear of nudity. (Ep. 7) The nephew learns what a grown man's testicles look like when he can't help but watch his uncle laboriously climb to the upper bed while wearing extraordinarily short cut-offs. (Ep. 27) This is before the boy's dad sends him to give his uncle a bath. (Ep. 47)

- When the father announces that he's having a prison love affair with an ice cream sandwich, he tries to toss a bite into his middle son's mouth. (Ep. 2) Missing personal contact, the father confides, "Daddy horny, Michael," and asks his son to arrange a conjugal visit. When the son encourages his mother to visit the prison, saying "He's lonely," she replies, "That's what his children are for." (Ep. 6) The daughter wears a top emblazoned with "SLUT" to visit her father in prison. (Ep. 8) When the parents finally enjoy conjugal relations, the eldest son can't help but watch. (Ep. 6)

- The mother and her brother-in-law have sex in her son's bedroom, on a hand-shaped chair. The son walks in on them, exclaiming, "Make love in your own hand, mother!" (Ep. 25) Speaking of hands, the youngest son's prosthetic hand gets used by his parents as a sex toy. "It's in the dishwasher," his mother says. "Your father and I were using it for something." "Oh for god's sake; can't you keep my hand to yourself?" The mother jokes with her middle son about the youngest: "He's just jealous that I have a man back in my life. And guess what else is back? My friskiness. Mama horny, Michael." "I'm amazed Dad hasn't strangled himself with his belt yet." "Oh, we're into all kinds of freaky scenes." (Ep. 42)

- The mother chides her middle son for not spending more time with her youngest: "Everyone's laughing and riding and cornholing except Buster.... You could pretend to be interested in him." Referring to his mother later, the middle son says, "She always has to wedge herself in the middle of us so she can control everything." The youngest son chuckles, saying, "Yeah, mom's awesome." However, in a Tourettes-like fit, he later calls her "an uptight b---- --- ----- [approximately three sentences are bleeped out]; You old horny slut!" Later, the mother interrupts a business meeting, brandishing candy at her youngest son: "Here's a candy bar. No, I'm withholding it. Look at me getting off." (Ep. 3)

- The son-in-law plays Cupid by rearranging the parts in a school play so that his nephew can kiss a male cousin (who is playing a female role). When his nephew quits the play, the son-in-law casts his own daughter in the male lead so that she can kiss her cousin. The nephew, George Michael, "watched as [his cousin] Maeby shared the kiss that should have been his with the boy he almost had to kiss. But to Maeby's surprise, she did not enjoy kissing [her cousin] Steve. 'You smell like my mom.'" (Steve is wearing his aunt's dress, you see.) (Ep. 3)

- The youngest son describes his new girlfriend to his brother: "I cannot tell you how liberating it is to be with someone who's not Mom." However, his girlfriend is his mother's age, shares her name, and is her best friend. (Ep. 4) Indeed, the girlfriend changed him as a baby. The mother puts her youngest son's bed in storage: "I guess you'll have to decide which Lucille you want to spend your nights with," to which he exclaims, "I'm going to continue dating, Mom," which sounds like "dating mom" and indeed "It's starting to feel a little like it." (Ep. 9) The youngest son eventually tells his girlfriend, "You're replacing my mother." (Ep. 12) After the youngest son stops dating his mother's best friend, the eldest son takes a turn, enticing her with the promise of elevating the knees of her Posturepedic bed. (Ep. 31)

- Undaunted, the mother prepares to participate in a charity bachelorette auction: "I think there's a certain bachelor who won't mind coming home with me at the end of the evening" (referring to her youngest son). The father, meanwhile, can't choose which prison gang to align himself with: "I feel like the prettiest girl at the dance." At the bachelorette auction, the middle son bids on and wins his sister. (Ep. 5) When the auction comes around again, the mother asks her middle son to bid on her and chides her daughter to find someone else because her brother is "bidding on mother." She later coaches her middle son how to compete with other bidders: "Start at five grand. If there are other bidders, back off gracefully. Shout out, 'I get her 364 days for free.'" (Ep. 31)

- Keeping it all in the family, the father's secretary/mistress has sex in a supply closet with the eldest son. (Ep. 6) Meanwhile, the middle and youngest sons lust after their older brother's "horny immigrant" girlfriend (with whom he sleeps in his mother's bed) until the older brother gives the middle brother permission to "Go for it." (Eps. 4, 7, 8, 12, 13) When the grandson asks his dad if he's dating the family's publicist, the dad says, "I'm absolutely not dating her. It's just you and me; Bluth boys." (Ep. 11) The granddaughter asks her uncle, "Why does everyone have to date, anyways?" He replies, "Isn't family enough for people?" The middle son announces to his son, "That cousin of yours is really something. Too bad you can't date her." (Ep. 25) The son writes an entire box's worth of love letters to his cousin. (Ep. 30)

- As an aside, the middle son hires a troupe of male strippers to teach his own son a lesson. (Ep. 10)

- The middle son shares his bed with someone for the

first time in years: his youngest brother. Later, he sleeps with his own son's ethics teacher, on whom the boy has a crush. The boy's aunt thinks her nephew wants a new mother and says, "I must say I'm a little hurt that you haven't considered me." The boy replies, "But you're my aunt." "That doesn't matter; aunts can fill that role, teachers can fill that role, and some day you're gonna find the right woman to fill that role, but till then, I'll be right across the hall." (Ep. 14)

- Upon being introduced to her newly adopted uncle, the granddaughter says, "So we're related; hey, do you want to go to a dance?" Her cousin mutters, "Great; another uncle to compete with." The granddaughter goes to the dance with her new uncle, only to ditch him for her cousin Steve. (Ep. 14)

- In prison, the father sells his son-in-law for a pack of cigarettes. (Ep. 18) The son-in-law licks his father-in-law's hand when shushed. (Ep. 35) The middle son calls his mother from the prison and asks her to tell his older brother that he's waiting for him: "I've got nice, hard cot with his name on it." She replies, "You'd do that to your own brother?" (Ep. 40)

- The oldest son's wife confesses, "I'm in love with your brother-in-law." He: "You're in love with your own brother? The one in the Army?" She: "No; your sister's husband." He: "Michael? Michael." She: "No; that's your sister's brother." He: "No; I'm my sister's brother. You're in love with me. Me!" She: "I'm in love with Tobias." He: "My brother-in-law?" She: "I know it can never be, so I'm leaving. I'm enlisting in the Army." He: "To be with your brother?" (Ep. 20)

- The middle son traditionally takes his own boy to "bring your daughter to work day," until he takes his niece. (Ep. 21) The boy is in touch with his feminine side and even volunteers to help with his uncle's "Sawing the Lady In Half" trick, playing the lady's legs. (Ep. 9)

- The youngest son pouts that his mother called her middle son to escort her to a soccer game, saying "I guess I'm not good enough to be her husband." The middle son questions his mother: "Why can't Buster pretend to be your escort; that's the way he's got it in all his cartoons." She explains, "They already know he's my son." When the middle son declines, she calls on her husband's twin brother. (Ep. 21)

- The daughter asks her twin brother, "I mean, how do you not have sex with me?" He responds, "It's a struggle." (Ep. 22) "And that's when Maybe decided to use her uncle to make her cousin jealous." (Ep. 23)

- The father's twin brother goes to bed with his sister-in-law. She worries aloud that her son will hear them making love. The twin brother replies, "That's what makes it so hot." Moments later, the son walks into the bedroom saying he heard "zoo noises" and the twin brother flagrantly displays his erect penis. (Ep. 24)

- The grandson whispers sweet nothings to his girlfriend, making his dad jealous he's not the target of the boy's affections. (Ep. 25)

- The son-in-law invites his brother-in-law to a dinner for two, noting, "If I blew myself early, I'll be nice and relaxed for a 9 o'clock reservation." (Ep. 25)

- The granddaughter tells her mother, "All Pop-Pop ever wanted was to see you with another man besides daddy." Her mother replies, "You're right. You know what? I'm gonna throw on a skirt, take off my underwear, and make your Pop-Pop proud." (Ep. 26)

- The father dresses in his middle son's dead wife's

maternity clothes, wears her perfume, and confesses that he used her old breast pump as a sex toy. (Ep. 27) Later, he hosts a play tea party with his granddaughters childhood dolls and asks, "Who wants to take their top off?" (Ep. 35)

- By the way, the family attorney asks the middle son to answer a "yes/no" question by tapping him on the fanny. (Ep. 27)

- The granddaughter tells her cousin Steve that her mom is actually her dad in drag; Steve finds himself attracted to the supposed transvestite and agrees to a lunch date. The granddaughter explains to her other cousin, "He's obsessed with her; that's all he wants to talk about. But it's only because he thinks she's got a penis. I told him she was a tranny." (Ep. 27)

- Acting as president of the family business and wearing his father's suit, the eldest son announces, "I did finally get into Dad's pants, though I had have the crotch taken in a little bit." (Ep. 28)

- At the office Christmas party, the middle son and his niece sing a karaoke duet of "Afternoon Delight," the rampant sexual innuendos ["The thought of rubbing you is getting so exciting"] shocking the entire staff. The next day, at another office party, the daughter and her nephew notice the middle son and his niece are "all over each other," so to make them jealous they sing a karaoke duet of "Afternoon Delight." The daughter's husband tells a flummoxed staff member, "That's my wife and my nephew; we have an open relationship." (Ep. 28)

- When the mother becomes tense in her husband's twin brother's absence, her husband tells his middle son that his wife needs to have sex with his brother. The middle son suggests that his uncle provide his mother with some "Afternoon Delight," to which he responds, "The question is which way do I try to get it in her? Maybe I'll put it in her brownie..." (Ep. 28)

- The mother appears on the cover of the Balboa Bay Window magazine with her youngest son for an article titled "Why I want to marry my mother." (Ep. 29) Later, the son hires a photographer for an update article entitled, "Keepin' It Fresh." The photographer comments, "Okay, I think we have enough of you two kissing." (Ep. 33) The mother attends the "Motherboy" event—a dinner dance aimed at promoting mother-son bonding—twenty-five times with her youngest son, and on a few occasions had won "Cutest Couple." As her son entered sexual maturity and she left it, it became harder to win. Now it's "Motherboy XXX." (Ep. 35)

- The youngest son needs a date for a dance, and the middle son suggests their mother. "I think the age difference is really starting to catch up to us," the youngest son explains. The brother-in-law cuts in: "My schedule is as open as my relationship with my wife. Why don't we pair up? . . . Even it means me taking a chubby, I will suck it up." The middle son interrupts: "Enough family stuff for today." Later, at a bar, when asked if there's a girl in his life, the youngest son replies, "Well, I would hardly call my mother a girl, but she's still very much a part of my life." (Ep. 30)

- The middle son wins a romantic weekend and invites his own son: "I thought maybe we could do it together; you know, sort of like a Valentine's present. . . . What do you say? We'e got a basketful of father-son fun here." His son picks up a bottle of Kama Sutra oil, next to edible body chocolate. The middle son's brother-in-law walks up, saying, "You really are quite the Cupid, aren't you. You can sling your arrow into my buttocks any time." Later, the granddaughter passes along a message to her uncle: "My dad wanted me to thank you for the romantic getaway; don't tell me what that means." When asked where her father is, she replies, "He left, dressed all Westerny; you can leave me out of that part, too." Her uncle walks off, exclaiming, "I screwed my brother-in-law." "Well, I'm all grown up now," says the niece. (Ep. 32)

- When the middle son tells his sister that he enjoyed three orgasms in a row with his childhood girlfriend, his sister is unimpressed, having just masturbated three times. (Ep. 32)
- The family solicits "Uncle Jack" to buy back shares of the company stock from a rival, luring him with the promise of sexual favors from either the mother or the daughter, at the father's suggestion and arranged by the middle son. (Ep. 32)
- Referring to the middle son's former lover, the eldest son says, "You know what I'd do? Have her pee in a cup. And have her pee in a cup right in front of me." (Ep. 33)
- The daughter and her husband rekindle their romance by making out while hidden in a shower at the middle son's girlfriend's house as they wait to surreptitiously collect her urine so as to determine whether or not she's impregnated with the combined sperm of an interracial gay couple. (Ep. 34)
- The youngest son confides that his mother likes to change clothes in private before asking to be zipped up, "yet anything goes at bath time." One of her garments has a zipper so long that her son has to get on his knees to start it. (Ep. 35)
- The mother catches the youngest son in bed with the maid and fires her, replacing her with a Roomba vacuum. Then she catches her son in bed with the Roomba. No one bats an eye when the son-in-law dresses in drag to work as the family's new

housekeeper, "Mrs. Featherbottom." (Ep. 36)

- At a party to celebrate his pre-engagement, the grandson catches his father making out "secularly" with his girlfriend's mother. Meanwhile, the boy's grandfather renews his wedding vows: "I will love and honor your spirit and flesh—first the flesh. I will caress and tweak; I will nibble and bite; I will blow, alternatingly hot and cool. I will always be here for you to rest your ankles upon my shoulders." The grandson's girlfriend gets hot flashes listening to the vows. (Ep. 38)

- The oldest son complains, "Well, gee, I didn't think the woman I'd be checking out at Spring Break would be Mom." The youngest son retorts, "She's better looking than the whores you date. . . . Mom's still got it!" What the mother wants, however, is to enjoy a spa weekend with her middle son: "I want to spend Spring Break with you." But first, she engages in a drinking contest with her husband's secretary, wagering a cooler containing 250 cc's of his "reproductive material." (Ep. 39)

- At the pier, the son-in-law challenges young male students on Spring Break to strip on camera while his wife films them: "Let's see some bananas and nuts. Perhaps we should just pull their pants off." (Ep. 39)

- The secretary and the brother-in-law both flash their nipples at the middle son in his office. He then sets the two of them up on a date, and they go to Vegas together. (Ep. 40)

- The middle son suggests that his mother take a date on a getaway to the family cabin in the woods while her husband is in prison. She asks, "How am I supposed to find someone willing to go into that musty old claptrap?" After three full beats, it dawns on the son that his mother is referring to the cabin. (Ep. 41)

- When the eldest son cries over being neglected as a child, he demands that the middle son taste his tears. "I'm not going to lick your eye." A minute later, when the eldest son is crying tears of happiness and embraces his brother for another lick, exclaiming, "Taste the happy," the middle son notes, "It tastes a lot like sad." (Ep. 41)

- When the middle son can't go camping with his own son, he suggests the boy "pop a tent in front with your cousin Maeby." When the cousin excuses herself as "not outdoorsy," her uncle says to his son, "This is a good chance for you to rub off on her." (Ep. 41)

- The granddaughter Maeby brags to her cousin George-Michael that she's "getting pretty serious" with her other cousin. "That Steve sure knows how to please a lady!" Masking jealousy, George-Michael responds, "I was hoping he would be gifted sexually. ... What a fun, sexy time for you!" Later, George-Michael discovers Steve naked and asleep in Maeby's bed. When he asks her what happened, she replies "I gave him a roofie. A girl's gotta grow up sometime." (Ep. 43)

- Apropos of nothing, the daughter announces to the family attorney (in front of his own daughter), "That's so funny, because I can put my leg behind my head!" (Ep. 44)

- The eldest son reveals how he wields his power as a beauty pageant judge, so that he can bed the third place contestant—a little bit plain but with super low self-esteem. The third place contestant turns out to be his nephew's girlfriend, a devout Christian, whom we find out the eldest son is dating. (Ep. 44) Later, the eldest son confides to the middle son, "I've got this Christian girlfriend, and she's trying to get me to become a better man and reconnect with my son, and I'm trying to get her to renounce God and f***

me, and I just want to prove to her that I'm worth it."
(Ep. 47) Meanwhile, the son-in-law introduces to his
wife a priest he met at the gym. The priest is carrying
a "Let Priests Marry" sign. (Ep. 50)

- The son-in-law challenges his nephew to have sex
  with his girlfriend while he watches. When the
  nephew is reluctant, the son-in-law tells the girl,
  "You need to decide whether you want a man or a
  boy. I know how I'd answer." (Ep 44)

- By the way, the son-in-law's business card reads
  "analrapist" [sic], his compound version of analyst
  and therapist. (Ep. 43)

- The father counsels at-risk young gay men at a
  fairground "Startled Straight" tent: "You want to be
  some guy's girlfriend? Want to have some guy reach
  you in the middle of the night, start messin' with
  your junk?" Someone asks, "Is he ugly?" "No—it's
  pitch black; you don't see him. It never stops, guys.
  And everybody acts like it's no big deal." "Is there a
  cover charge?" "There's nothing to do all day except
  lift weights, fold laundry. Get thrown into a cage
  with a bunch of sweaty men." (Ep. 44)

- The middle son's fiancé, a mentally retarded female,
  defiantly announces her engagement to her uncle.
  He's concerned: "It's not your fault your parents
  were cousins, but here we are. I've been charged with
  taking care of you, and I'm bloody well gonna do
  it!" She answers, "Michael will be my cousin soon
  enough, because we're getting married." (Ep. 46)

- The daughter says to her twin brother: "You
  may not like it that Mom has needs, but it never
  bothered you when Dad was running around."
  He replies, "That was different." She then asks,
  "Well how about when she was sleeping with Uncle
  Oscar?" "The guy looks just like Dad—I don't
  know, he's family, it seemed only natural they'd

be together." Anxious about the impact of this statement on the grandson's taboo relationship with his cousin, he asks "What is natural? Is there new legislation on this now?" (Ep. 47)

- While on a date with her husband's prison warden, the mother calls her daughter asking her to deliver a tube of vaginal lubricant. (Ep. 47)
- During a tight embrace, the eldest son (who has a magician's dove hidden in his crotch) tells his middle brother "If you feel something moving down there, it's just the bird;" however the middle son sees that the bird has escaped, thus proving that the eldest brother is sexually aroused. (Ep. 48)
- After his sister glues the broken thumb back onto his prosthetic hand, the youngest son lashes out against his uncaring mother: "Sister's my new mother, mother. And is it just me, or is she looking hotter, too?" "Why don't you marry her?" "Maybe I will!" (Ep. 49)
- In a televised mock trial, the son-in-law asserts that he knows nothing because he spends "so much time making sweet love on my wife that it's hard to hear anything over the clatter of her breasts." (Ep. 50)
- Days earlier, the middle son awakens to find his teenaged son in his bed. The boy was there in fear of "the monster called lust"—his lust for his cousin, with whom he made it to "second base," having gone in "head first like Pete Rose." Later, the middle son awakens to find his twin sister in his bed, drunk. He broaches the subject of their respective children's physical relationship, which prompts her to straddle him, exclaiming that she's only his adopted sister. "I know you've always found me attractive; you've been telling me that for the last 40 years." The next morning, the middle son awakens to find his brother-in-law in his bed. "You can't

spoon me like that," the middle son says. (Ep. 53)

- When he learns that his sister was adopted and plans to marry her middle brother, the eldest brother hits on her at a party: "Why go for the best when you can go for the rest ... of your life with a younger man?" Oh, and the middle son awakens to find his father in bed with him. (Ep. 53)

- The middle son makes a date with a prostitute he thinks may be his long-lost twin sister. He "felt a connection like he'd never felt with anyone in his family." He offers her a job at the family business, handling the entire staff: "you're going to be filling like three openings." When asked about her specialty, she says, "I do all sorts of scenes." He entreats the staff to put her into "any position you want." He doesn't yet realize that her pimp is his older brother's hand puppet, but when he does, the brother offers him a "family discount" and then mutters, "Maybe I should be getting a family rate." (Ep. 51)

And what does this family call its act?

- The "Arrest-ocrats."

The Top Ten Unpaintable Blues

- The far mountains of Bertraghboy Bay, Ireland. "In the intense cold of late evening the further shores of Bertraghboy Boy seemed to catch and hold the last of the sunlight, the seawrack below high-water line glowing orange, the walled fields above burnished green, the far mountains an unpaintable blue." (*The Crying of the Wind*)

- The New Mexico desert sky. "I awoke in the desert of New Mexico to behold golden sand, golden grass, green-gold sage brush, golden wastes, vast, craggy, creviced, cliff-sided buttes rising turret-like, a wide domain bounded by purple mountains and unpaintable blue sky." (Robert Jackson, *Montreal Gazette*)

- Twilight in the California desert. "Strewn from the western desert's wild wings across the unpaintable blue of the twilight sky stream rose-red pennants, tender yet resplendent—not the washed out hue of other sunset skies but the soul satisfying glory of color the desert sky alone can show." (*The Desert and the Rose*)

- The mountains of Moab. "The intense blue belt of water beyond, terminating in the clear, soft tones of the indescribable, unpaintable blue mountains of Moab." (*Excavations at Jerusalem, 1894-1897*)

- The shore of ancient Kamiros, Rhodes. "You look down from the central plinth across a winding main street backed by the taut hard unpaintable blue of the sea, and the smoky chunks of the Turkish mainland." (*Spirit of Place: Letters and Essays on Travel*)

- The Azorean ocean. "Then there is the intense blue of the Ocean. I have never seen such deep, completely unpaintable blue before. It is so different from the opaque grayish waves that hit the coast of Holland." (Pieter Adriaans, "Painting on the Azores")

- Someone other than Brittany's irises. "She can't see any tiger gold or unpaintable blue in Brittany's irises." ("Full Moon on a Sunday Night," Part One)
- The sky over Portland, Oregon. "The air is crisp and the sky is unpaintable blue." (Scott Conary)
- The blue sky anywhere. "Ruskin says that a blue sky is unpaintable — blue fire he calls it, and unpaintable — and yet Australians cannot accept this." (*Plein Airs and Graces: The Life and Times of George Collingridge*)
- The Huxtable kitchen. "[I]n all its badly-hung, unpaintable, powder-blue glory." (Andy Peters)

There's nothing so comfy as mediocrity. Indeed, our culture teaches us both explicitly and implicitly that "okay" is good enough. But when it comes to fun, the middle-of-the-road game players cheat themselves out of something precious. Lackluster players miss out on the special spark that characterizes outstanding game play. We're not talking about the thrill of victory versus the agony of defeat. An outstanding player will have more fun losing a game than an average player will have winning a game. The fact is that mediocre players cannot, by definition, get caught up in the lighthearted spirit of the game.

Following are ten techniques for transforming yourself into an outstanding player of your favorite game.

Top Ten Tips for Run-of-the-Mill Players to Enjoy Outstanding Games

- Seek your game's hidden source of entertainment, its heart of fascination. In Classical times, Greek and Roman games consisted mainly of running, wrestling, jumping, riding, and racing. On the surface, these games were nothing out of the ordinary, yet their players made them the world's most extraordinary entertainments, exciting the enthusiasm and awakening the spirits of the spectators.[1] To find your game's heart of fascination, observe those moments when players become carried away, when they exclaim joyously, when they leap into the air or rise off their seats as if suddenly weightless. Notice those moments when teams cheer one another, when the thrill of the play dissolves rivalry. When you identify the dynamic at play—the true spirit of the game—you can foster it, prolong it, and take it to Olympic heights.

- Improve your flexibility and agility (whether muscular or mental). To stretch your gray matter, a Web search for "lateral thinking exercise" will offer puzzles unsolvable by traditional step-by-step logic. To increase your physical flexibility, the "sun salutation" of Yoga is a 12-step series of poses that exercise every muscle and joint of the body. Do a Web search for "sun salutation" to find free pictorial guidance.

- Use drills to work on weaknesses (whether muscular or mental). If another player is one step ahead of you mentally or one second faster than you physically, that's a winning edge. A single increment of improvement may be all you need for success. Set simple goals and work one step at a time.

- Better your memory. A good memory is a boon to virtually any game. A Web search for "memory game" will yield hundreds of free online resources for exercising your powers of recollection.

- Dispel falsehoods that hinder you. Are you convinced that golf isn't a woman's game, or that softball is a young person's game, or that pinball is about making lights blink with a rolling ball? Educate yourself about your game. Read books, explore websites, talk to other players. There's always more to learn.

- Sharpen your concentration. This is the age of the eleven-second attention span. Being easily distracted is ruinous to game play. Sharpening your concentration takes conscious, prolonged, repeated effort. Keep a journal about your game. Thinking and writing about your game will help to increase your power of concentration.

- Manage your stress. Stress management techniques will help you improve virtually any game. A

Web search for "stress management" will yield hundreds of free online tips and techniques. One marvelous stress reducer is laughter. A Web search for "laughter therapy" will inform you about how laughter reduces stress hormones, boosts immunity, promotes a positive attitude, and engenders a feeling of power.

- Practice solo. If your game involves two or more people, don't let that fact discourage you from practicing any aspects you can work on by yourself.
- Embrace change. "Change is necessary to improve your game. You must not be afraid to risk giving up the known for the unknown if you wish to play better."[2]
- The final tip is too specific to apply to just any game. You already know what it implies, or will soon discover it through your ongoing self-education. Perhaps this tip will require the help of a coach or the advice of a teaching pro. Perhaps it will involve visualization techniques, or the use of a video camera, or familiarization with quantum physics. This final tip may be the ultimate key to your fullest enjoyment of your game.

Notes:

[1] Lewis Henry Morgan, *League of the Ho-dé-no-sau-nee Or Iroquois*, 1904, p. 303.
[2] Philip B. Capelle, *Play Your Best Pool*, 1995, p. 383.

18 Meanings of the word OOO

In the Japanese superhero series *Kamen Rider OOO*, the word OOO has at least eighteen distinct meanings:

- infinity with an additional circle or infinity times the letter O (as written in cake icing in episode one of the series; referred to in the theme song as "Skip the addition—multiply your way up").
- the unstoppable progression of the idiom "anything goes" (referred to in the theme song as "Anything goes, goes on: ooo's, ooo's, ooo's, ooo's").
- one thousand (the letter O's symbolizing zeros, as the series sports the one-thousandth episode of the Kamen Rider franchise).
- three medallions (referring to an ancient coin-shaped technology for artificial life that acquired consciousness; the three coins are inserted into the hero's belt to trigger a transformation).
- the name of a masked hero (sometimes also spelled Os, pronounced like the oes in *goes*).
- multiple kings (from the Japanese pronounciation *Ozu*).
- a joyous bouquet (an allusion to the idiom that "everything is coming up roses," referred to in the theme song as "Coming up OOO").
- the "three of pentacles" in the Tarot (symbolizing coordinating with others, finding all the needed elements, functioning as a unit, cooperating, meeting goals, knowing what to do and how to do it, and proving one's ability, as per *Learn Tarot*).
- rarity (as in the old Celtic "Chant of Arcady" sung at harvest gatherings: "I'll sing the three O's. What means the three O's? Three, three's the rare O!"

—A. S. Harvey, *Ballads, Songs and Rhymes of East Anglia*, 1936, page 107).

- a winning move ("A single line of three 'O's is worth more than anything because a move that produces this result is a winning move!" —Mike James, *Artificial Intelligence in Basic*, page 30).

- omnipotence, omniscience, and optimization ("The three O's, omnipotence, omniscience, and optimization ... continue to appear in modern times in the way we conceive of ourselves through the social sciences. Mortal beings figuring out how to act in the world are routinely modeled as if they have unlimited computational power, possess complete information about their situation, and compute the optimal plan of action to take." —Peter M. Todd & Gerd Gigerenzer, *Ecological Rationality: Intelligence in the World*, pp. 496-7).

- outflanked, outfoxed, overwhelmed ("The 'Three O's': a defence must be either Outflanked, Outfoxed, or Overwhelmed." —*Current Research on Peace and Violence*, 1987, page 129).

- continual practice ("Whenever anyone asks why our name is spelled with three O's, we remind them that to be good at picking there is no other path than to practice Over and Over and Over again." —*Deviant Ollam, Practical Lock Picking*, 2012, page xi).

- the possibility of different combinations ("The three O's tempt the reader to explore the possibilities of different combinations." —Guillaume Apollinaire & Anne Hyde Greet, *Calligrammes*, 1908, page 407).

- decimalization ("For every three O's added to the given number, we shall have one place of decimals. And, in general, since the nth power of ten has no O's we shall always have, in extracting the nth root, one place of decimals for every n O's added to the given number." —Silas Totten, *A New Introduction to the Science of Algebra*, 1836, page 225).

- a belt, as in the three stars of the constellation Orion. ("The three o's [are part of a] densely woven mesh of triplets [that] constellates this moving poetic object." —Michael Golston, *Poetic Machinations*, 2015).

- rising to a challenge ("As soon as the ball is served, the three O's come out to challenge." —Jacob Daniel, *The Complete Guide to Coaching Soccer Systems and Tactics*, 2004).

- seizing the day; embracing the world ("The three o's are a circular microcosm of the day, or, of the world." —Robert Greer Cohn, *The Poetry of Rimbaud*, page 60).

Duties of the Attendant of the Borgesian Circulating Depository

I am an Attendant of the Borgesian Circulating Depository. My duties are:

- honoring visionary ancients who were centuries or millennia before their time
- tilting the game board so as to cast everything in a new light
- celebrating allegory and metaphor as scenic shortcuts to wisdom
- discovering the macrocosm in the microcosm;
- measuring non-material forces which nonetheless carry weight (Umberto Eco)
- tracking extraordinary tempests in mundane teacups
- inding mystical analogues to scientific breakthroughs—putting the super into the natural, the other into the worldly, the meta into the physical, the para into the normal, the magical into realism
- puzzling over hidden, deeper meaning
- carrying the key, even when the lock has been lost;
- identifying archetypes at play
- studying the legend, even when the map is blank;
- searching through the deepest shadows for the bright light that cast them
- delving into the unfathomable in wordless awe of the inexplicable
- photographing background images for the insides of mystery boxes

- offering the inscrutable its due scrutiny
- endowing branches of Borgesian catacombs
- diagramming the sacred syllables in the mumbo jumbo
- believing as many as six impossible things before breakfast
- building 3D models of M.C. Escher's visual illusions
- crafting something out of nothing
- designing floor plans for memory palaces
- plundering cultural detritus
- bringing warmth to fuzzy logic
- looking through trompe l'oeil windows
- freeing radicals
- centering on marginalia
- navigating the ocean that roars within the seashell
- making the past perfect and the future less tense
- seeking a grand unification of hard science, soft science, and ethereal science
- resisting the belligerence of ignorance
- erecting signs on dotted lines
- taking a stand for poetic justice
- tracing constellations in the starry-eyed
- fighting to cure anhedonia
- getting in stitches over how many angels can dance on the point of a needle
- exploring intangible powers, from those celebrated by the world's great religions to square roots to the literary tradition (Umberto Eco)
- directing good brain power to fanciful ends.

Rejected album titles

A band in England once asked me for weird words for album names, but they ended up not taking any of my suggestions. (Sad.) I suggested:

- *Eellogofusciouhipoppokunurious* (meaning "very good," from a slang dictionary of the 1930s)
- *Pentadecylparatolylketone* (the chemical composition of limelight)
- *Poluphlosboiothalasses* (from *Punch* magazine, 1859 ... I don't recall what it means)
- *Hysterico Vaporous Hypo Megrins* (a fictional diagnosis for a condition in which one is unstuck in time; the patient is lost to the present even as the future and the past loom up before his half-closed eyes. This phrase appears in a poem entitled "Heroic Treatment," by a certain G.A.K., printed in *Harper's*, Aug. 1887).
- *Vercingetorix Chilblains* (a phrase that delivers zero web search results, from *Purple Parrot*, 1923).
- *Krikketekrakkle* (a monstrous insect mentioned only once in history, in *Judy, Or The London Serio-Comic Journal*, 1878).
- *Ypzneml* (the name of a steam-powered automaton, in *The Harvard Lampoo*n, 1887).
- *Whizzerinktums* (a word we've found only in *Medical Pickwick*, 1920).
- *Anti-prosopopoeia* (meaning being against figures of speech in which an abstract thing is personified or an absent or imaginary person is represented as speaking; from 1815).
- *Xlvcd* (a word written on a wall by spirits with a candle, it translates as, "Spirits of a higher order

desire to communicate with you soon." From *Modern Spiritualism* by Eliab Wilkinson Capron, 1855).

- *Twigmuntus, cowbelliantus, perchnosius* (a phrase from *Fairy Tales from the Swedish* of G. Djurklo, 1901).
- *Crinita draconibus* (having dragons for hair; haired with dragons. From *Four Books of the Metamorphoses of Publius Ovidius Naso, Expurgated and Freed From Everything Objectionable* by Nathan Covington Brooks, 1890)
- *Zmiolwxyzmu* (a word referring to "kissing exhibitionism" and other public displays of affection, from a headline in *Daily Tar Heel*, 1940).
- *Gedämpfteerwartungenenttäuscht* (the awful realization that one's colleagues are as bad as one's students; this word appears only in *The Musubi Murder*, by Frankie Bow)
- *Phrenaeleonogopolae* (a word that appears only in *Toike Oike*, 1966).
- *Rolyksnolyb* (this word comes down to us via a short story by L. Ron Hubbard, *Unknown*, 1941).
- *Druckfehlerteufelchen* (the name of the typo gremlin, from *Nebelspalter*, 1938).
- *Hullawhaloopity* (a word that appears only in *The Gateway*, 1975).

My transliteration of made-up words in *The Strange World of Gurney Slade*

- kerplotschk
- splillge
- formansville
- spoogle-crene
- spumatz
- spinglehaute
- flangewicke
- klittervithe
- hendlecraw
- mandeltheau
- pendlewean
- pattybah

Given my substantial research into esoteric tomes, I'm sometimes consulted for strange and unusual magical spells. An award-winning quarterly magazine of art and culture based in New York [name withheld for reasons of discretion] once asked me for a spell to cast over their printing press. Most recently, a winner of two Gertrude Stein Awards in Innovative American Poetry [name withheld in a nod to our lost age of privacy] asked me for no fewer than thirteen different spells.

13 Magic spells I've been asked for

- A spell which finds and locates the source of (malicious) gossip and renders the "first tongue" of this gossip chain either serpent-like (i.e. forks the tongue) or like that of some other loathsome beast.
- A spell which will allow a refrigerator to enchant the food in it, so that when you eat the food you see the food's history (such as the worker picking the grapes. This would be quite grisly when it came to lunch meat and we realized it had a "family life.")
- A spell which will render water capable of transmitting its memories. When an enemy steps into a tub of "blissful" water, suddenly he or she is overcome with a thousand television stations of water memory, all the way back to the time of the dinosaurs.
- A spell that turns pussy willows back into the cats they once were.
- A spell which allows you to enter into a painting or use a painting, drawing, etc. as an avenue of escape.
- A spell to send snow back upwards into the sky—a reverse snowstorm spell.
- A spell to make someone fall in love with his or her own reflection. For example, a teenager cannot

concentrate in class but must constantly seek a reflective surface to the point of madness. Good for a stuck up kid in school, beauty queen hex, etc.

- A spell whereby you can have birds carry a message to other birds to so on to other birds in order to reach someone far away.
- A spell which makes someone the reverse of a money magnet, so money is always figuratively (and literally) flying away from him or her.
- A spell whereby planes flying overhead will drop valuable things into your yard or on your roof, like a form of tribute from airplane.
- A spell to turn pancake batter into quicksand, so when the person eats the finished product, the pancake inside the person slowly causes the person to implode into himself/herself, vanishing throughout the day in a very geometrically weird way.
- A spell on cookies to make them like online cookies; they drop without the eater's consent and glow, leading you to the person you are trailing and to whom you have given the bewitched cookie.
- A spell to make tornados play music. Needles appears within and the tornado is turned into an old school record player even as it grinds away at a landscape.

The whichness of the what

A headline read, "When the whichness of the what is really only a well-drained drip" (*The Gateway*, 1970). While reminding ourselves of the origin of "the whichness of the what," we encountered these variations:

- The whichness of the what and abstract ain'tness of the not, and the correctness of the is. (Norris Clarion Sprigg, *Sprigs of Poetry*, 1907)
- The Whichness of the What, as compared to the Thatness of the Thus. (G. E. Farrow, *The Wallypug of Why*, 1895)
- The whichness of the what and the whitherness of the wherefore. (Elsie Lincoln Benedict & Ralph Paine Benedict, *How to Analyze People on Sight*, 1921)
- The whichness of the what and whereforeness of the why. (The Evening Statesman, 1903)
- The whichness of the what—the howness of the when—the whereness of the whatever. (*The Gateway*, 1930)
- The whichness of the what of which nothing is any whicher. (Eben Leavitt, 1938)
- The Whyness of the Wherefore and the Whichness of the What. (*Georgetown Daily*, 1909)
- The whichness of the what and all that sort of thing. (*Buffalo Morning Express*, 1919)

Questions I asked the voices in our spirit radio

- What is on the dark side of the moon?
- Were extraterrestrials at play in ancient Egypt?
- Is the universe a hologram?
- Is there life on Mars?
- Is time an illusion?
- What is at the bottom of a black hole?
- Can we live forever?
- What is the universe made of?
- How did life begin?
- Is the end of the world imminent?
- Are we alone in the universe?
- What is consciousness?
- Why do we dream?
- What's so weird about prime numbers?
- Is there such a thing as free will?
- Are we being monitored by extraterrestrials?
- What is the secret of Area 51?
- Is time travel possible?
- What makes us human?
- Are there pyramids on Mars?
- Does the legendary continent of Atlantis exist?
- What is the secret of UFOs?
- Can you tell us about Bigfoot?
- Are poltergeists ghosts or demons?
- Are there aliens among us?
- What's at the bottom of the ocean?
- Are there pyramids on the moon?

- Where does a missing sock go?
- What is the secret of crop circles?
- Is the nature of these spirit voices angelic or demonic?
- Does the flat earth theory hold water?
- Is there an objective reality?
- What should we know about quasars?
- What is the nature of the chupacabra?
- Can you reveal a secret of astral / out-of-body travel?
- Does the Flat Earth theory hold water?
- Can you tell us about crystal skulls?
- What of the Hollow Earth theory?
- What is the secret of unicorns?
- What is the face on Mars?
- What should we know about UFOs?
- What should we be doing now?

101 ways I failed to reduce vinegar

- Couldn't handle the fumes.
- Couldn't risk evaporation (high price per ounce).
- Balked at our pretentious refinement (chichi).
- It somehow turned back into wine.
- Cultural appropriation.
- Always feel irritated when told to "simmer down."
- A bout of acerophobia.
- Wouldn't know how to drizzle it, anyway.
- Gave up after an hour.
- Watched the pot.
- No clear advantages.
- Couldn't be bothered.
- Pot cracked.
- Couldn't get the cork out.
- Milkman called.
- Forgot dinner-guests.
- Couldn't afford the time.
- Reached the bottom of the barrel.
- Couldn't risk scalding.
- Forgot to add vinegar.
- Stove temp. too low (211°).
- Couldn't justify taking the trouble.
- Mistook steam for bubbles.
- Recipe didn't call for it.
- Feelings of uneasiness.
- Can catch more flies with honey.
- No time to gather firewood.

- Hired careless servant.
- Voices said not to.
- Didn't have two sticks.
- At triple point.
- No amount of wishful thinking.
- Utilities deliquent.
- Too busy watching paint dry.
- Resisted overcooking.
- Forgot to remove the pot's lid.
- Indifference.
- Wasn't trying to.
- Adverse vapor pressure.
- Where to begin?
- Too busy bleeding turnip.
- Trickle-down economics.
- Don't know how.
- Raw food diet.
- Global cooling.
- Don't care for glazes.
- Forgot to pre-heat.
- Hot flashes.
- Plastic spoon melted.
- Pot not compatible with induction cooktop.
- Couldn't take the heat.
- A series of intangibles.
- Already let off my steam.
- Can't follow simple instructions.
- Enthusiasm dwindled.
- Not on my fad diet.

- Doubted thermodynamics.
- Prefer Green Goddess dressing.
- Customary admonitions.
- Old-school environmentalist.
- Lost the recipe.
- Failed minimum requisites.
- No aptitude.
- It was already drizzling outside.
- Still in rehearsals.
- Failed Home-Economics.
- Doctor's orders.
- Just married.
- All fingers and thumbs.
- Rolling blackouts.
- Wrong place and time.
- Kettle fit for dungheap.
- A general conspiracy.
- Better things to do.
- Inauspicious horoscope.
- God's will.
- Gone fishin'.
- Not enough energy.
- High altitude.
- Not on the Sabbath.
- Stage 3 restrictions.
- Too many cooks.
- The clock stopped.
- Peer pressure.
- Afraid of nutrient loss.

- Spring fever.
- Blew a fuse.
- Burned midnight oil.
- Blasted whirly-gigs.
- Sour grapes.
- Eating out more often.
- The inner saboteur.
- Absentee charwoman.
- Ex-husband got the kitchen.
- Don't eat boiled vinegar.
- Perfectionism.
- Viscous cycle.
- Bout of blennophobia.
- Nothing to go with it.
- Tried to cut back.
- My salad days were over.

Yes/No Questions for a homemade lie detector

- Your wish is that I wish what you secretly wish.
- Within a two-hour period, you have eaten an amount of food that most people would consider excessive.
- You've ruled out the possibility that you're being overly suspicious.
- You know who she is and she knows what she is.
- That time you said you loved the chocolate cake, you threw up a little in your mouth.
- The fact that you tend to stay up through the hours of darkness has nothing to do with a craving for blood.
- When you lie you break out in a rash.
- You pray to be forgiven for doing that thing with the thing.
- There's just no explaining that whatchamacallit.
- You secretly dream of waking up as a Canadian.
- Maybe it's time to stop not doing what you pretended you can do and can't, and start doing the thing that you can't do but can no longer pretend that you can.
- Your secret desire is my deepest fear.
- You can't listen to very much Wagner because you start getting the urge to invade Poland.
- You're so busy with work that you don't have time to "give back to society."
- You have neither the money nor the know-how to get that thingamajig out of your head.
- You've ruled out deranged psychopathy and decided it sounds like fun.

- Nobody knows what you carry about with you in your pocket.
- No one will ever suspect that you have the whatsit in your possession.
- Your secret desire is to bust out that straw-cowboy-hat-and-flip-flops look without looking out of place.
- You have drunk champagne out of the slipper of a dancing girl.
- You want to live better than you do now and work fewer hours.
- You did not mean what you said that day we parted.
- You have a playroom all to yourself.
- You want to found a new religion.
- Though talkative and often high-strung, your secret desire is to be with someone to whom you don't have to say a word, someone whose eyes are hypnotic and whose arms are soothing and strong.
- You secretly dream of being in front of the camera.

51 Yearbook Motifs Bingo

Invite partygoers to bring an old yearbook. Participants trade yearbooks. Call out a motif, a point going to the first person to find and display a matching photo. Game ends with the first paper cut. The 51 motifs listed here are the very most common running themes in yearbooks, so this is a game more about speed than luck.

- skull (human or animal)
- same photo duplicated within yearbook
- person studying at the end of library shelves corridor
- human pyramid
- woman hugging a tree
- man sunbathing
- mop or yarn wig
- person in a trash can or dumpster
- Groucho glasses with mustache
- man being thrown into a body of water
- toilet or urinal, unoccupied
- person sitting on toilet
- parking ticket on automobile
- fraternity brother being paddled
- "artistic" double-exposure photo
- person donating blood
- men in comedy drag
- burning building
- kitten or cat
- racial stereotype costume
- man asleep on a park bench or common room sofa

- picket/protest sign
- group of men wearing ties but no pants
- face and/or body covered in shaving cream
- car bashed with sledgehammer
- man holding snake
- sign on a door
- mud-covered buddies embracing
- adult wearing a diaper
- pie in the face
- man on the phone
- person behind bars or otherwise caged
- candle- or torch-wielding hooded figure
- thespian man applying makeup in a mirror
- reading an upside down book
- man wearing only a towel
- clock tower
- student holding vinyl record
- two or more men in bed together
- effigy
- camera-shy person holding hand or book to face
- man shaving
- face painted as skull
- silhouette
- men kissing
- person posing next to a tombstone
- skeleton with a cigarette in its mouth
- man sticking hotdog or banana into his mouth while staring at the camera
- streakers

- athlete's wounded foot being bandaged
- single face or scene reduplicated by kaleidoscopic lens

Both Samuel Taylor Coleridge and Samuel Coleridge-Taylor ...

- wrote about Kubla Khan
- had romantic natures
- were Englishmen
- are known for musical rhythm
- displayed natural abilities
- were of frail health
- were instrumental in helping others find their own voices
- had "veins uncontaminated with one drop of Gentility"
- died too young
- continue to be popular

www.ingramcontent.com/pod-product-compliance
Lightning Source LLC
Chambersburg PA
CBHW031416210526
45464CB00005B/1911